Complete Study Edition

Chaucer's Canterbury Tales
the Prologue

| Commentary | Interlinear Text | Glossary |

edited by
SIDNEY LAMB
Associate Professor of English,
Sir George Williams University, Montreal

INCORPORATED
LINCOLN, NEBRASKA   68501

D0858905

ISBN   0-8220-1404-1

Copyright © 1966
by
C. K. Hillegass

All Rights Reserved
Printed in U.S.A.

Chaucer's Canterbury Tales
the Prologue

CHAUCER WAS NEVER MORE MEANINGFUL—

. . . than when read in Cliff's "Complete Study Edition." The introductory sections give you all of the background information about the author and his work necessary for reading with understanding and appreciation. The inviting three-column arrangement of the complete text offers the maximum in convenience to the reader. Each line of Chaucer's original poetry is followed by a literal translation in simple modern English. Adjacent to the text there is a running commentary that provides clear supplementary discussion. Obscure words used by Chaucer are explained directly opposite to the line in which they occur.

SIDNEY LAMB—

. . . the editor of this Chaucer "Complete Study Edition," attended Andover Academy and Columbia University. He was graduated from McGill University, receiving the Prince of Wales Medal for Philosophy and the Moyes Travelling Fellowship. Following graduate studies in Elizabethan literature at King's College, Cambridge, from 1949 to 1952, he became a member of the English Faculty of the University of London's University of the Gold Coast in West Africa. Professor Lamb joined the faculty of Sir George Williams University, Montreal, in 1956.

Chaucer's Canterbury Tales
the Prologue

Contents

The Scribe

HIS LIFE

We sometimes tend to think of poets as living outside the pressures and problems of every-day life, concerned only with artistic creation in a remote world of their own. Nothing could be less true of our first great poet, Geoffrey Chaucer. He lived at the center of the affairs of his day, having been, among other things, a soldier, a courtier, a royal emissary to Europe, a controller of customs, a justice of the peace and a member of parliament. We might have expected such a career from the artist who gave us rich and varied portraits of his contemporaries from every walk of life: knight, innkeeper, miller, monk, and all the rest. They were created by someone continuously and sensitively in touch with the life around him.

We cannot positively date Chaucer's birth but the evidence suggests he was born between 1340 and 1344 in London. His father, John Chaucer, a minor official in the court of Edward III, was the vintner responsible for the transmission and disposal of the wines for the various royal households. We may imagine the effect on the imagination of his young son, who must have spent much of his time at the wharves, watching

Travelers at an Inn

Studying the Word of God

...tion to Geoffrey Chaucer

the unloading of the great casks of "the wyn of Spaigne that crepeth subtilly," or the "whyte wine of Oseye [Alsace] and red wine of Gascoigne," and listening to the strange stories of the sailors from France and Spain, and the tales of the British dockhands. Chaucer's introduction to the rank and file of the society which he was later to use as his material in *The Canterbury Tales* began early. John Chaucer's position was a respectable one, and his son was awarded a position of page in a household of royal rank—that of Prince Lionel, one of the sons of Edward III. Although the exact extent of Chaucer's education is unknown, to be a page in such a household was a preparation for entrance into court society, and it was a thorough and valuable education. The young Chaucer would have been exposed to French and Latin (which were, respectively, the languages of the court and church), and he would have encountered the elegant code of manners and the elaborate ceremonies of court life.

In 1367 Chaucer was receiving a pension as a yeoman or groom in the king's household and by 1368 he is recorded as an "Esquire" in the king's retinue, which indicates a significant advancement. The court of Edward III comprised the highest personages of the realm in political power, and in intellectual and artistic prestige. Chaucer was now in a position where he would be exposed to exalted figures and have some peripheral part in the great events of his day. It is perhaps surprising that, rising as he had from the vintner's-son-become-page to a place of prominence, that he did not lose his understanding of the common people. We know from the *Canterbury Tales* that he did not, and from some of his other writings, that he was always able to view the aristocratic environment with objectivity and something like ironic tolerance. Chaucer remained—and we may be thankful for it—primarily a poet. Whatever his involvement in the stirring business of the court, he never lost the observant, perceptive qualities of the artist.

In 1366 he married Philippa de Roet, a lady in attendance on the queen, and about this period began a series of foreign missions as the court representative. More importantly, these travels served to enlarge his experience and bring him into fruitful contact with the European literature of his day. French culture was already familiar, French still being the language of much court and diplomatic business, and French literature widely read and admired. It was Italy that provided the most stimulating literary experience for Chaucer. Italy has always exerted an important influence on the English poets, through its vivid color and Mediterranean sunlight as much as through its poetry, and this was as true in the fourteenth century as it was to be again in the sixteenth and the nineteenth. Chaucer probably had a reading knowledge of Italian before he first went to Italy, and by the time of his second visit (in 1378) he was certainly proficient in the language. There he was to receive strong doses of Dante, Petrarch, and Boccaccio, from whom he learned and borrowed. These authors had forsaken classical Latin and French to write in their native Italian. Chaucer adopted the idea and wrote in the current Middle English. The foreign excursions are largely responsible for what critics call Chaucer's "French" and "Italian" periods, and they include some of his finest poems: *The House of Fame, The Parliament of Fowls, The Legend of Good Women,* and *Troilus and Criseyde.* But Chaucer's greatest work is reserved for his last, or "English" period.

Chaucer was by this time an important official: in 1382 he be-

Various Paraphernalia from the 14th to 15th Century Period

came controller of petty customs, in 1385 justice of the peace for the county of Kent, and in 1386 a knight of the shire (member of parliament). Suddenly, through some complex shifts of power in the court, he was deprived of all his offices. He regained favor later, but we may be thankful for this political setback of 1386, since it gave Chaucer the leisure he needed. Having digested and assimilated the literature of France and Italy, the "English" period now begins with the composition of *The Canterbury Tales*. We may, by the same token, regret Chaucer's return to public service, since he was never able to finish them. He died in October 1400 and was buried in Westminster Abbey. An impressive tomb was erected over his grave in the fifteenth century, and this section of the Abbey became the burial place for the great English writers to follow Chaucer, and is called Poets' Corner. There could be no more fitting place for the grave of the Father of English Poetry.

HIS WORLD

The technological differences between our age and Chaucer's are obvious enough when we think of the weird astrological-medical theories of the "Doctour of Phisik" (*Prologue* 411-44), or of the fact that it took Chaucer's pilgrims three days of hard travel to traverse the sixty miles between London and Canterbury. The differences in society and its assumptions are impor-

tant in understanding the actions and attitudes of Chaucer's pilgrims.

The social structure of England (and all Europe) in the fourteenth century was feudal, that is to say power radiated from the king, through his nobles (when he could control them), and through their subjects, with little kingly power reaching the lower echelons of society. The king and his nobles owned the land, which was divided into great agricultural estates, and these provided the men, material, and money which supported the crown and its wars. Society was organized in a hierarchical form, one's wealth and power being a matter of what position one occupied on the hierarchical ladder. This ladder extended from the king, through the great noblemen-landlords (like Chaucer's patron, John of Gaunt, Duke of Lancaster), down through lesser landlords and their various executive officers with, at the bottom, the serfs who worked the land for their masters. It is perhaps important to note that while we may regard this system as unjust and oppressive, the medieval people could conceive of no other. Each level of society had its rights and privileges, and each had its duties and obligations. Despite the occasional abuse they regarded the system as right and proper.

Three groups of Chaucer's pilgrims may be isolated to suggest how this system worked. The

first represents agricultural feudalism (the first and basic kind) founded on land ownership and service. The Knight, who is highest on the scale, is a landowner, and has therefore served in the wars for his king, and he will be followed in this by his son, the Squire. The Knight's Yeoman is a servant, whose only duty is to the Knight. The Franklin also holds land, perhaps "in fee" from some noble, but more probably in his own right. His service is the direction of his farm, his obligation to the noble or king being doubtless in the form of the yearly harvest, and of men in time of need. The Miller does not himself own land but has been given the right to mill all grain on an estate; the Reeve manages an estate. They are both servants, but of an exalted kind, and make shrewd and profitable use of their power, as we shall see. The lowest in the hierarchy is the Plowman, who simply tills the land.

England was changing in the fourteenth century, and one of the most important changes was the growth of a new, urban society (mainly in London) where the feudal structure was somewhat modified. Neither the Doctor nor the Sergeant of the Law owned land, although they were both men of substance. The Doctor (Chaucer tells us) made money out of the plague, and the Lawyer made money out of almost everything. They were the beginning of a new class, today

Virgin and Child

called professional men. The Manciple and the Merchant and even the Wife of Bath (who is a clothmaker) also represent the urbanization process. They were not directly commanded by anyone, and in time they became the mercantile middle class who overthrew the monarchy and the last vestiges of feudalism in the civil war of the seventeenth century. It is also significant that the Haberdasher, the Carpenter, the Weaver, and the Dyer are presented together, in that they are all members of one of the great parish guilds. It was through these craft and parish guild associations that the new urban artisans achieved the power that they lacked through not belonging to the land-hierarchy.

There is yet a third group, constituting a kind of feudal system of its own, and representing one of the most powerful elements of medieval society— the church. Nine of Chaucer's thirty pilgrims belong to the clergy, and it would be difficult to overestimate the importance of the Roman Catholic church to the lives of the people of western Europe in the fourteenth century. They might disregard its teaching (as some of the pilgrims do) or complain of its abuses (as Chaucer does) but from baptism, through confirmation and marriage, to the funeral rites, it was intimately connected with their lives. It was a visibly potent force throughout England, from the great cathedrals—such

as Canterbury—and the religious houses, down to the humble parish churches.

Despite the worldly aspects of life that so often appear in *The Canterbury Tales* we should not forget that the people Chaucer gathers together are pilgrims, and that the occasion for their gathering is the spring pilgrimage to the shrine of "the holy blisfil martir," St. Thomas Becket, at Canterbury. We can gauge the importance of the church in men's lives by noting how many varieties of belief or simulated belief Chaucer presents. They run all the way from the dedicated holiness of the Parson, through the superficial observances of the Prioress, to the outright hypocrisy of the Summoner and Pardoner. Chaucer, looking about him, sees fit to define a large proportion of his characters by where they stand with regard to the church.

It is sometimes suggested that the medieval world was a happier, simpler, and less troubled time than our own. In some ways this is true—certainly Chaucer's pilgrims are free from many of our modern anxieties— yet the fourteenth century had its own troubles, and it is an oversimplification to regard it as a time of innocent good humor. In fact it is the overall good humor of Chaucer's treatment that has fostered this view, and while he is basically optimistic, he would be unlikely to accept it.

The plague, or Black Death (to

which Chaucer occasionally alludes) entered England in mid-century with dreadful consequences. It is said that half the population was wiped out, and while this may be an exaggeration, it is no exaggeration to say that medieval man lived in constant fear of its ravages. One of the effects of the plague was to inflate prices and further depress the already grim living conditions of those at the bottom of the economic ladder. This in turn produced the insurrection known as the Peasants' Revolt (1381), in which the infuriated mob murdered a good many of those whom they regarded as their exploiters. Chaucer—as a justice of the peace and a member of parliament—might be expected to be bitter about this unprecedented attack on the social order. It may be a measure of his magnanimity that only a few years after the rebellion his portrait of the Plowman in the *Prologue* is remarkable for its praise of the peasant virtues.

The Hundred Years War continued, with the French threatening to invade England; this is one of the reasons for the warlike nature of Chaucer's Shipman, whose merchant ship was obliged to be a fighting vessel, and it also accounts for the Merchant's anxiety about trade if the shipping route between Middleburg in the Netherlands and Orwell in England is broken.

The church itself was divided at the time, one faction having a pope at Rome and the other at Avignon, with some of Europe (including England) supporting the first and some (including Scotland) the second. The confusion resulting from this situation was probably in part the cause of the clerical abuses that produced so much complaint (some of it in the *Canterbury Tales*) during the period.

If we set these disruptions alongside the achievements of art and literature, the security of a stable society, and the calm that comes from faith (the qualities usually presented as typical of the Middle Ages), we shall probably be somewhere near the truth. At any rate it was a time of transition and great variety: an appropriate time for the creation of a work as varied and multicolored as *The Canterbury Tales*.

9

The Martyrdom of Saint Thomas Becket

an introduction to

POETIC BACKGROUND

Although we are dealing here with the *General Prologue* to *The Canterbury Tales,* something must be said about the whole work to which it is an introduction. *The Canterbury Tales* is a series of stories bound together by· a frame (as it is usually called) which gives unity to the whole work. There are various ways of placing a group of stories within some unifying frame. The individual stories may be connected by a central character (as in *The Adventures of Sherlock Holmes*) or by a continuing situation (as in the *Arabian Nights' Entertainment*), and it is the latter that *The Canterbury Tales* most closely resembles.

The frame is, of course, the pilgrimage which brings the characters together. In Chaucer's case the device is exceptionally useful, since it would only be possible to bring the representatives of the various classes together socially on such a pilgrimage. In this way Chaucer is able to create the contrasts and oppositions between his various characters that make *The Canterbury Tales* such a broad study of humanity.

The tales themselves are dramatic and there is a good deal of dramatic development among the characters. The Miller, drunk, insists on telling his tale out of turn, and this tale then infuriates the Reeve, since it seems to be a slur on his own person. The Shipman flatly refuses to hear a sermon-tale from the Parson, and so on.

The *Prologue* simply introduces these figures, briefly and brilliantly sketched. The greatest virtue of Chaucer's poetry may be its swift and subtle suggestion of a whole character through a few carefully selected details. "I see all the pilgrims," wrote Dryden, "as distinctly as if I had supped with them at the Tabard in Southwark."

Let us look at some of the stylistic devices Chaucer used to get his characteristic effects. The first thing that strikes us about the style of the *Prologue* is its easy, conversational quality. This is perfectly appropriate since Chaucer *is* telling us a story, and he frequently injects a phrase to remind us that we are listening to a narrator's speaking voice: "Of Norfolk was this Reve *of which I telle,*" or "Ful fetys was hir cloke, *as I was war.*" The same trick is at work in those conversational, careless phrases (and Chaucer takes great care

10

14th Century Inn

the Prologue

to seem careless) such as "this is to seyn" and "forsooth," as we might say "you see" or "get this!" The effect is not of reading a dead poem but of listening to a live, spontaneous voice. Chaucer also likes to give his characters popular phrases. Thus the Monk laughs at the text, or rule, of his monastic order. "He yaf nat of that text a pulled hen," and later, "but thilke text heeld he nat worth an oystre," and we feel the immediate, downright quality of the Monk's mind through his speech.

Compression is one of poetry's fundamental techniques and in Chaucer it takes the form of communicating the quality of a character in a brief, suggestive phrase. The dainty Prioress (whom we suspect of being a snob) sings "the service dyvyne/ Entuned in her nose ful semely," and we can almost hear her. If the Miller cannot tear a door from its hinges he would "breke it at a rennyng with his head," and the almost comic exaggeration suggests the man's clumsy violence. There is also the self-important Lawyer, who was doubtless a busy man, "And yet he semed bisier than he was," and the young Squire, so perpetually in love that "He slept namoore than dooth a nyghtyn-gale," and the scholarly, selfless Clerk, "And gladly wolde he lerne and gladly teche."

The *Prologue* is, among other things, comic poetry, and humor is one of Chaucer's favorite ways of delineating character. Often this takes the form of a tongue-in-cheek pretense on Chaucer's part that he is a simple and impressionable man. At one point, apologizing to the reader for the unskillful way he is about to present matters, Chaucer writes, "My wit is shorte, ye may wel understonde." Thus he seems to take some of his pilgrims—especially the ones that are pleased with themselves—completely at their own valuation. The Doctor is without peer in his profession, "In al this world ne was there noon hym like," and so is the Shipman, "There nas noon swich from Hulle to Cartage," while the Manciple could direct the household "Of any lord that is in Engelond." Of course these apparent inflations of reputation are really deflations because they are accompanied by a sly Chaucerian wink. Here Chaucer is only making gentle fun of his pilgrims' pretensions, and this sort of praise must be distinguished from the kind he bestows upon the characters of whom he either thoroughly dis-approves or approves. When he outlines the evils of the Summoner, for example, and goes on to say, "A bettre felawe sholde men noght fynde," his amiability has turned to bitter satire. On the other hand, he regards the Parson with unqualified admiration and the line "A bettre preest I trowe that nowher noon ys" means just what it says. In every case the context makes the meaning of the individual phrase quite clear.

One of the best general criticisms of Chaucer was written by one of England's earliest critics, the poet-dramatist John Dryden. This is what he says about the poetic representation of character in *The Canterbury Tales*:

He must have been a man of a most wonderful comprehensive nature, because as it has been truly observed of him, he has taken into the compass of his *Canterbury Tales* the various manners and humours (as we now call them) of the whole English nation in his age. Not a single character has escaped him. All his pilgrims are severally distinguished from each other; and not only in their inclinations, but in their very physiognomies and persons.... The matter and manner of their

"Sitting under the Word"

The Pilgrimage to Canterbury

tales, and of their telling, are so suited to their different educations, humours and callings, that each of them would be improper if in any other mouth. Even the grave and serious characters are distinguished by their several sorts of gravity: their discourses are such as belong to their age, their calling, and their breeding; such as are becoming of them, and of them only. Some of his persons are vicious, and some virtuous; some are unlearn'd, or (as Chaucer calls them) lewd, and some are learn'd. Even the ribaldry of the low characters is different: The Reeve, the Miller, and the Cook are several men, and distinguished from each other as much as the mincing Lady-Prioress and the broad-speaking, gap-toothed Wife of Bath. But enough of this; there is such a variety of game springing up before me that I am distracted in my choice, and know not which to follow. 'Tis sufficient to say, according to the proverb, that here is God's plenty.

TRANSLATION

The Canterbury Tales were written around the period 1387-1400, and the English language has changed a good deal since that time. It has not changed so much, however, that the reader who is prepared to spend a little time cannot recover a great deal of the full flavor of Chaucer's English. With a little study and a little practice he will find himself at home with Chaucer's sound and meaning, versification and form, and will get a good deal of pleasure in becoming familiar with Chaucerian turns of phrase and tartness of expression.

This edition of the *Prologue* provides both an interlinear translation and a glossary, so there should be no trouble in understanding what Chaucer is saying. However, one point about the change of word meanings between the fourteenth and twentieth centuries ought to be made. The difficulty with a word may arise because the word is completely unknown to us: it has simply dropped out of the language (e.g., "bismotered" for stained) and here the reader need only look at the translation or glossary.

A different sort of difficulty arises when we come across a word in Chaucer which we still use, but with a quite different sense. For example when we read that the Friar is "a ful solempne man," we understand "solempne" to be our "solemn" (which it has become), but this seems hardly the word to apply to the gay Friar. We have lost the word's original meaning— "festive"—which it takes straight over from the Latin. There are a good many words like this in Chaucer, where what seems to us the obvious, modern meaning is not the Chaucerian meaning, and the reader has to watch for them.

SOUND

Scholars have been able to reconstruct the approximate sounds of Chaucer's language. Since he was a poet who meant his work to be read aloud, we ought to be able to hear, if only with the ear of the imagination, how his lines sounded. For an extensive list of the phonetic differences between current pronunciation and that of the fourteenth century, consult either the Robinson or Baugh editions given in the bibliography. However, there are three rules which will give a reasonable rendition of Chaucerian spoken English.

1. Pronounce all written consonants as we do in modern English. However, *gh* as in *night*, is pronounced like the *ch* in the Scottish *loch*, a guttural sound unfamiliar in English. Knight is pronounced *nicht*.

2. Pronounce all the syllables in a word, even the final *-e*, which should be lightly stressed. Chaucer's *dame* was pronounced *dah-meh*, and *dames* was *dah-mess*.

3. Pronounce all written vowels in the way in which they would be pronounced in modern French or Italian. Thus Chaucer's *page* has an *a* pronounced *ah*, like the *a* in the French *plage*, so *page* is pronounced *pahj-eh*. Chaucer's *fame* is *fah-meh*, *name* is *nah-meh*.

Pronounce the vowel spelled *e* or *ee* in Chaucer's *regioun* as the *ay* sound of modern French *region* (or modern English *rate*).

There are exceptions to this, but the main point is that Chaucer's *e* is pronounced *ay* as in *may* not *me*.

Pronounce the vowel spelled *i* or *y* in Chaucer's *fine* as the *ee* sound in modern French *fine* (or English *machine*).

Pronounce the vowel spelled *ou* or *ow* in Chaucer's *doute* as the *ou* sound in modern French *doute* (or modern English *soup*).

VERSIFICATION

Understanding the metrical structure of Chaucer's lines is important and fortunately this is fairly simple. In most of *The Canterbury Tales* (and in the *Prologue*) Chaucer used the rhymed iambic pentameter, or five-beat couplet, later to become famous (with Dryden and Pope) as the heroic couplet. The important thing here is to discover, by experimental reading, how the five beats fall in the line. The experimental element lies in discovering the changed accent in some words, and in others whether or not the final -*e* is to be sounded. As an example of the first, take the line

He hadde maad ful many a mariage.

We are tempted to say

He had made full many a marriage,

which spoils Chaucer's five-beat rhythm. Sound the final -*e* in *hadde,* and notice the unfamiliar accent in *marriage* and the line will read, correctly,

He hádd-e maad ful mány a marríage.

In the line

She hadde passed many a straunge strem,

we are tempted to say,

She had passed many a strange stream.

The failure to sound the final -*e* makes this metrically incorrect. The metrically correct version is

She hádd-e páss-ed mány a stráung-e strém.

After a little reading of Chaucer's iambic pentameter the reader begins to distinguish easily between the mute and the sounded final -*e*.

FORM

Some of Chaucer's grammatical forms and constructions are strange to us. Here are some of the more frequent differences between Middle and Modern English: Pronouns are the same as in modern English with the chief exception of two ambiguities. The word variously spelled *her, here, hir, hire* is Chaucer's equivalent of the modern *her* and *their.* Chaucer's *his* is the equivalent of the modern *his* and *its.*

Most verb forms resemble their modern counterparts, but the following four peculiarities should be noted. Chaucer normally uses the form (*he, she, it*) *loveth* rather than the modern verb form *loves.* Verbs with stems ending in -*d* or -*t,* how- ever, regularly contract the ending -*eth,* thus appearing as *he bit* (for *biddeth*), fint (*findeth*), *holt* (*holdeth*), *stant* (*standeth*).

Many verb endings had a final -*n,* now gone, which might be dropped. Thus *we* (*ye, they*) *love* and *loven* are used interchangeably for modern *we love; we lovede*(*n*) for modern *we loved;* and *to love*(*n*) for modern *to love.* Also optional was the prefix *y-* as a sign of the past participle, so that modern *I have loved* appears sometimes as *I have y-loved,* and *I have drunk* as *I have y-dronke*(*n*).

One sign of the negative was *not* or its variants *noght* and *naught.* Another sign was *ne* or *n',* which was often accompanied by other negative words. "He nevere yet no vileynye *ne* sayde/ In al his lyf unto no maner wight" means literally, "He never yet no villainy didn't say to no kind of person", i.e., he never yet spoke any villainy to any kind of person. *Ne* combines with the word that follows in the frequently occurring sequence *nadde* (*ne hadde,* "hadn't"), *nere* ("weren't"), *nolde* ("wouldn't"), *noot* (*ne woot,* "know not"), *nyl* ("will not"), *nyste* (*ne wiste,* "knew not").

13

Bibliography

EDITIONS

Baugh, A. C., ed. *Chaucer's Major Poetry*. Appleton-Century-Crofts, 1963. Contains all the *Canterbury Tales* as well as the rest of Chaucer's most important poems. Notes and glossary are excellent.

Manly, J. M., and E. Rickert, eds. *The Text of the Canterbury Tales*. 8 vols., Chicago University Press, 1940. The definitive modern edition, with variant readings, and extended notes and glossary.

Robinson, F. N., ed. *The Works of Geoffrey Chaucer*, Houghton Mifflin, 1957. The best one-volume edition of the complete works, with full introductions and notes to the individual poems.

COMMENTARY AND CRITICISM

Bennett, H. S. *Chaucer and the Fifteenth Century*. Oxford University Press, 1947. A thoroughgoing treatment of the literary and social background.

Bowden, Muriel A. *Commentary on the General Prologue to the Canterbury Tales*. Macmillan, 1948. Extensive background material on the characters who appear in *The Prologue*.

Chute, Marchette. *Goeffrey Chaucer of England*. Dutton, 1946. A popular account of Chaucer's life.

Coghill, Nevill. *The Poet Chaucer*. Oxford University Press, 1949. Scholarly and authoritative treatment of poet's career.

French, R. D. *Chaucer Handbook*. Appleton-Century-Crofts, 1947. Useful notes on each of Chaucer's works with the emphasis on factual detail rather than critical evaluation.

Lowes, J. L. *Geoffrey Chaucer*. Indiana University Press, 1958. A very perceptive critical analysis.

Trevelyan, G. M. *Illustrated English Social History, I: Chaucer's England and the Early Tudors*. Longmans, 1949. A valuable study of Chaucer's social and cultural background.

the Characters

THE KNIGHT . . . . an honorable warrior who fought for Christianity against the heathen.

THE SQUIRE . . . . the knight's son; a lusty youth.

THE YEOMAN . . . . . servant to the Squire.

THE PRIORESS . . . . . worldly superior of a nunnery, accompanied by another nun and three priests.

THE MONK . . . . a fat, bald, lover of hunting and luxury who rejects work or study.

THE FRIAR . . . . a merry monk who is an accomplished beggar for his own gain.

THE MERCHANT . . . . . a pompous businessman who talks honestly while actually practicing illegal moneylending.

THE CLERK . . . . the threadbare scholar who prefers philosophy to riches.

THE SERGEANT . . . . . one of a select group of lawyers, equal to the Knight in social status.

THE FRANKLIN . . . . . a wealthy landholder and civic leader fond of excellent food.

THE HABERDASHER, CARPENTER, WEAVER, DYER, TAPESTRY MAKER
wealthy tradesmen; members of the same parish guild.

THE COOK . . . . the private cook for the Parish Guild members.

THE SHIPMAN . . . . . . an accomplished sailor and drinker.

THE DOCTOR . . . . . . a learned practitioner with a love for gold.

THE WIFE OF BATH . . . a vivid, gap-toothed widow who has enjoyed many pilgrimages and five marriages.

THE PARSON . . . . a poor, diligent cleric who aids parishioners with his own funds.

THE MILLER . . . . a wealthy, broad, and brawny tradesman; talkative and bawdy.

THE MANCIPLE . . . . . a shrewd kitchen supervisor.

THE REEVE . . . . the crafty manager of a lord's property.

THE SUMMONER . . . . . a lecherous cleric who permits parishioners' licentious behavior—for a price.

THE PARDONER . . . . . The Summoner's companion who sells allegedly holy relics and pardons from Rome.

MYSELF . . . . the poet who accompanies the pilgrims and recounts the tales.

THE HOST . . . . the commanding, genial innkeeper who proposes that each pilgrim tell two stories on the road to Canterbury and two on the return journey.

THE SCENE: . . . . *Tabard Hostelry, Southwark, England.*

THE PROLOGUE

[Lines 1-20]

The Prologue opens with an evocation of the season. It is spring, and the bleakness of winter has given away to the renewal of natural life (nature is personified at 11), and the "droghte" of March to the "flour" of new growth. This passage is more than simple scene painting, or a pleasant preliminary to the introduction of the characters. It has a symbolic value, for the renewal is also in the human world, one manifestation being the pilgrimage to a holy shrine. Spiritual as well as animal and vegetative life is revived and there is a parallel between the three sorts of life. The "tendre croppes" are once more "inspired" and the "smale foweles maken melodye" and in the human world "longen folk to goon on pilgrimages." Chaucer always presents man as part of the natural world, and here the desire for spiritual replenishment (no matter how unspiritual some of the pilgrims turn out to be) is part of the universal, recurrent renewal of nature.

The pilgrimage had become, by the fourteenth century, a popular form of excursion for some (as the presence of the Wife of Bath suggests) and it also included the whole spectrum of society, from Knight to Plowman, which is convenient for Chaucer since it allows him to bring together a good many socially disparate types. As the roads and inns improved through the century pilgrimages became less dangerous and therefore, for some, less of a dedicated spiritual act. For many of Chaucer's pilgrims the food and wine and the exchange of stories is as important as any spiritual fulfillment. Chaucer gives us both aspects of the pilgrimage, and the "gloutenie," "drunkennesse," and "falsnesse" of some of his group is contrasted with the "worthynesse" and "reverence" of others. Chaucer is both narrator and one of the imagined pilgrims, and he meets the others at the Tabard Inn, in Southwark, to begin the journey.

In Chaucer's day Southwark was a small suburb of London, south of the Thames, and nothing like the dense urban area it is today. It was the chief road to the southern counties and the ports and famous for its inns, and the Tabard was one of the best, appropriate for the "nyne and twenty" visitors.

St. Thomas Becket (or à Becket) as Archbishop of Canterbury opposed Henry II over the balance

GENERAL PROLOGUE

To the Canterbury Tales

Chaucer

Here Bygynneth the Book of the Tales of Caunterbury

Whan that Aprill with his shoures soote   1
When April with his showers sweet

The droghte of March hath perced to the roote,
The drought of March has pierced to the root,

And bathed every veyne in swich licour,
And bathed every vein in such liquor,

Of which vertu engendred is the flour;
Of whose virtue is engendered the flower;

Whan Zephyrus eek with his sweete breeth   5
When Zephyr too with his sweet breath

Inspired hath in every holt and heeth
Has made alive in every grove and field

The tendre croppes, and the yonge sonne
The tender sprouts, and the young sun

Hath in the Ram his halfe cours yronne,
Has in the Ram his half course run,

And smale foweles maken melodye
And small birds make melody

That slepen al the nyght with open yë—   10
That sleep all night with open eye—

So priketh hem Nature in hir corages—
So Nature goads them in their hearts—

Thanne longen folk to goon on pilgrimages,
Then people long to go on pilgrimages,

And palmeres for to seken straunge strondes
And palmers to seek strange shores

To ferne halwes, kouthe in sondry londes;
To far-off shrines, known in various lands;

And specially from every shires ende   15
And specially from every shires' end

Of Engelond to Caunterbury they wende,
Of England, to Canterbury they wend,

The holy blisful martir for to seke
The holy blessed martyr to seek

That hem hath holpen whan that they were seeke.
Who helped them when they were sick.

Bifel that in that seson on a day,
It happened that, in that season on a day,

In Southwerk at the Tabard as I lay,   20
In Southwark, at the Tabard as I lay,

3. "veyne": sap-duct.
"licour": life-giving moisture.

4. "vertu": here, the power to make grow.

5. "Zephyrus": the west wind, often associated with spring.

8. "Ram": the first division, or sign, of the zodiac (Aries), hence the sun is called "yonge," since it has only entered the first stage of its annual course (March-April).

10-11. i.e., springtime amorousness causes the birds to sing all night.

13. "palmeres": pilgrims, so called from the palms that they carried.

15. "shires": one of the political-geographical divisions of England.

16. "Caunterbury": site of the shrine of St. Thomas.

17. "martir": Archbishop Thomas Becket, whose feud with King Henry II led to his murder in 1170. The scene of this martyrdom was the object of pilgrimages for centuries afterward.

20. "Southwerk": a borough of London on the south side of the Thames.
"Tabard": an inn, identified by a sign showing a "tabard," a short coat worn over armor. The plowman on the pilgrimage is wearing a "tabard" (see 541).

17

THE PROLOGUE

[Lines 21-44]

between royal and ecclesiastical power. They had been friends, and then enemies. Their opposition, and its outcome, has been the subject for several dramas in our own time. Henry had made Becket archbishop, but instead of using his ecclesiastical power to support the monarch, Becket took his obligations seriously, and excommunicated several of Henry's supporters who had traduced the authority of the church. They appealed to Henry, who, it is reported, was seized with anger and cried out that "a fellow that I loaded with benefit dares insult me, and tramples on the whole kingdom! . . . what cowards have I up in my court, who care nothing for their allegiance to their master! Will no one rid me of this turbulent priest!" Four of his knights set out for Canterbury, where they murdered Becket in the cathedral. The man whom many had regarded as worldly and arrogant was, soon after his murder, regarded as a martyr and later canonized as a saint. His blood was held to contain great curative qualities, restoring health to the sick, and small quantities of it (diluted, and apparently inexhaustible) were given to pilgrims to Canterbury for centuries after.

The Knight is the first of the pilgrims to be introduced. This is doubly appropriate, since the Knight stands at the top of the social hierarchy in this gathering and since he is a virtuous character

Redy to wenden on my pilgrymage
Ready to travel on my pilgrimage

To Caunterbury with ful devout corage,
To Canterbury with a fully devout heart,

At nyght was come into that hostelrye
At night there came into that inn

Wel nyne and twenty in a compaignye
Full nine and twenty in a company

Of sondry folk, by aventure yfalle   25
Of sundry folk, by chance fallen

In felaweshipe, and pilgrimes were they alle
Into fellowship, and pilgrims were they all

That toward Caunterbury wolden ryde.
That toward Canterbury would ride.

The chambres and the stables weren wyde,
The chambers and the stables were large,

And wel we weren esed atte beste.
And well were we treated with the best.

And shortly, whan the sonne was to reste,   30
In brief, when the sun had gone to rest,

So hadde I spoken with hem everichon
I had so spoken with them, every one,

That I was of hir felaweshipe anon,
That I was forthwith of their fellowship,

And made forward erly for to ryse
And made an agreement to rise early

To take oure way ther-as I yow devyse.
And take our way, as I shall tell you.

But nathelees, whil I have tyme and space,   35
But nevertheless, while I have time and space,

Er that I ferther in this tale pace,
Before I further in this tale proceed,

Me thynketh it acordaunt to resoun
I think it reasonable

To telle yow al the condicioun
To tell you all about the nature

Of ech of hem, so as it semed me,
Of each of them, as they appeared to me,

And whiche they weren, and of what degree,   40
And who they were, and of what rank,

And eek in what array that they were inne;
And also in what clothes they were dressed;

And at a knyght than wol I first bigynne.
And with a knight then will I first begin.

A Knyght ther was, and that a worthy man,
A knight there was, and he a worthy man,

That fro the tyme that he first bigan
That from the time that he first began

State shoe

The Knight

18

THE PROLOGUE

[Lines 45-67]

and embodies a standard of behavior against which some of the subsequent characters may be judged and found wanting.

Today we look back on knighthood, chivalry, and "curteisye" as romantic and unreal. It is true that few could live up to the rigorous aspirations of the orders of knighthood, yet as a code of behavior it did exist and Chaucer, who never shows any desire to whitewash or improve his characters, presents the Knight as a real representative of the code. The origins of the knightly ideal lay in Pope Urban's proclamation of the first crusade, at the end of the eleventh century. His motive was to "bring those who wastefully wage private wars" into the service of Christendom against the "infidel and barbarian." The pope's requirement for these soldiers was that they be "wise, provident, just and pure." They were not only to be champions of the church, but also protectors of the weak, and exemplars of moral virtue.

The list of the places in which the Knight had fought would have a romantic ring to Chaucer's readers. Christendom in the fourteenth century was relatively small, and circumscribed by "heathenesse"—mysterious lands and peoples described by the occasional traveler. Yet the Knight's campaigns are all real enough. They have been divided by historians into three groups, chronologically. The first includes the long struggle to expel the Moorish (Saracen) invaders from Spain. Alfonso of Castile besieged the city of Algeciras ("Algezir") in the kingdom of Castile for almost two years, and only after terrible hardship was it taken from the Moors. There were many English knights in this besieging force, under the earls of Derby and Salisbury. The war was subsequently carried into north Africa, against "Belmarye" and "Tramyssene," in the 1340s and 1360s, the latter well within the memories of many of Chaucer's readers. One source speaks of a challenge issued by the Saracen nobles to the Christian knights to engage in individual combat—possibly a reference to the "lystes" in which the Knight had "slayn his foo." The second group of campaigns ("Alisaundre . . . Lyeys . . . Satalye") occurred in "the Grete See"—the eastern Mediterranean and Asia Minor. King Peter of Cyprus was in command of these, and in preparation he toured all of Europe to secure men, ships, and supplies.

To riden out, he loved chivalrye,   45
To ride forth, he loved chivalry,

Trouthe and honour, fredom and curteisye.
Truth and honor, generosity and courtesy.

Full worthy was he in his lordes werre,
Full worthy was he in his lord's war,

And therto hadde he riden, no man ferre,
And in these he had ridden (no man farther),

As wel in Cristendom as in hethenesse,
In both Christian and in heathen lands,

And evere honoured for his worthynesse.   50
And was ever honored for his worthiness.

At Alisaundre he was whan it was wonne.
At Alexandria he was, when it was won.

Ful ofte tyme he hadde the bord bigonne
Many a time he had headed the table

Aboven alle nacions in Pruce;
Over those of all nations, in Prussia;

In Lettow had he reysed, and in Ruce,
In Lithuania he had fought, and in Russia,

No Cristen man so ofte of his degree.   55
More than any other Christian of his rank.

In Gernade at the seege eek hadde he be
In Grenada, too, he had been at the siege

Of Algezir, and riden in Belmarye.
Of Algeciras, and ridden in Benmarin.

At Lyeys was he, and at Satalye
At Ayas was he, and at Adalia

Whan they were wonne; and in the Grete See
When they were won; and in the Great Sea

At many a noble armee hadde he be.   60
With many a noble expedition had he been.

At mortal batailles hadde he been fiftene,
In fifteen mortal battles he had engaged,

And foughten for oure feith at Tramyssene
And fought for our faith at Tlemcen

In lystes thries, and ay slayn his foo.
Three times in the lists, and always slain his foe.

This ilke worthy knyght hadde been also
This same worthy knight had also been

Somtyme with the lord of Palatye   65
Once with the lord of Palatia

Agayn another hethen in Turkye.
Against another heathen in Turkey.

And everemoore he hadde a sovereyn prys;
And evermore he had a noble reputation;

45. "To riden out": i.e., take the field, go on military expeditions. "chivalrye": knighthood.

46. "curteisye": in addition to modern meaning of courtesy, the word in the Middle Ages implies the manners supposed to belong to the court.

51. "Alisaundre": Alexandria, captured by King Peter of Cyprus in 1365. The battles which follow indicate the Knight's long and distinguished military career. All the campaigns were against the infidels—Saracens, Turks, and pagans of northeastern Europe (Russia and Lithuania). See Commentary.

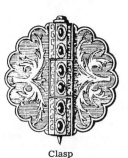
Clasp

58. "Lyeys . . . Satalye": in Armenia and Asia Minor, respectively; both were taken by Peter of Cyprus.

62. "Tramyssene": or Tlemcen, was in Algeria.

63. "lystes": lists or tournaments, meaning single combat against the enemy.

THE PROLOGUE

[Lines 68-90]

Alexandria was a rich and beautiful city, and considered impregnable, but the Christian forces took it, as one source says, "in a massacre unequalled since Pharoah." The third group in which knights from everywhere in Christian Europe were involved took place in "Pruce," "Lettow," and "Ruce," that is to say, on the border of eastern and western Europe. The Teutonic Knights had long been in conflict with the non-Christian peoples to the east. The ceremonial referred to as the "bord" of "Pruce" (52-53) was that of the Teutonic table of honor, a ritual assembly of knights at which those who had acquitted themselves well (like Chaucer's Knight) were placed at the head.

The Knight is a man of maturity and dignity, and by way of contrast, Chaucer now turns to his son the Squire, characterized by youthful enthusiasm. The language suggests his vivid quality: he is "embrouded" with "fresshe floures whyte and reede," is represented as "syngynge," and is, in general, "as fressh as is the month of May."

The Squire has had some military experience, but in the main his character is defined in terms of the various accomplishments traditionally expected of the well-born young man. There was, of course, proficiency in horsemanship and combat. The "juste" at 96 refers to jousting, in which two mounted opponents charged each other with lances. Jousting usually formed a part of some larger ceremony, such as a coronation, and gave the squires the chance to exhibit their ability with horse and lance. Contemporary accounts suggest that jousting was always dangerous and sometimes fatal for the participants. The arts of peace were as important as the arts of war. The Squire is skilled in "flotynge" and "daunce." The "daunce" was not unlike the folk dances that we know. The dancers joined hands and executed some fairly intricate steps under the direction of a leader who usually sang a song, the dancers

And though that he were worthy, he was wys,
And even though he was valiant, he was wise,

And of his port as meeke as is a mayde.
And in his manner as modest as a maiden.

He nevere yet no vileynye ne sayde   70
He had never uttered any vileness

In al his lyf unto no maner wight.
In all his life to any kind of person.

He was a verray, parfit, gentil knyght.
He was a truly perfect gentle knight.

But for to tellen yow of his array,
But to tell you of his dress,

His hors were goode, but he was nat gay.
His horses were good, but he was not gaudy.

Of fustian he wered a gypon   75
Of coarse cloth he wore a doublet

Al bismotered with his habergeon,
All stained by his coat of mail,

For he was late ycome from his viage
For he had lately come from a voyage,

And wente for to doon his pilgrymage.
And went to make his pilgrimage.

With him ther was his sone, a yong Squier,
With him was his son, a young Squire,

A lovere and a lusty bacheler,   80
A lover, and a lusty aspirant for knighthood,

With lokkes crulle as they were leyd in presse.
With locks curled, as though from a curling iron.

Of twenty yeer of age he was, I gesse.
About twenty years old he was, I guess.

Of his stature he was of evene lengthe,
In stature he was of average height,

And wonderly delyvere, and of greet strengthe.
And wonderfully agile, and of great strength.

And he hadde been som tyme in chivachye   85
And he had been once in the cavalry,

In Flaundres, in Artoys, and Picardye,
In Flanders, in Artois, and Picardy,

And born him wel as of so litel space,
And bore himself well, considering his short service,

In hope to stonden in his lady grace.
In hope of standing in his lady's grace.

Embrouded was he as it were a meede,
Embroidered was he like a meadow,

Al ful of fresshe floures whyte and reede.   90
All full of fresh flowers, white and red.

Sword Carriage

79. "Squier": esquire, whose candidacy for knighthood includes attending upon a knight, as here.

The Squire

86. "Flaundres...": a reference to the expeditions into Flanders, Artois, and Picardy as a part of the war between the rival popes of Rome and Avignon.

THE PROLOGUE

[Lines 91-113]

responding with the refrain. Finally, the reference to the nightingale would be clear to the fourteenth-century reader, since the bird was traditionally associated with love. Like sleepless young men before and since, the Squire was "in hope to stonden in his lady grace."

The position of knight required an attendant squire and a servant as well, which accounts for the Yeoman. In the fifteenth century the term yeoman came to mean a small landholder, but for Chaucer it meant a servant or attendant, in this case with the function of "forster." A "forster" was concerned with game rather than the preservation of the forest, and so the Yeoman wears a "hood of grene" (Lincoln green being the hunter's color) and carries a "sheef of pecock arwes." He has the accouterments of a hunter (and notice how carefully Chaucer has observed them—the sword and buckler, the dagger, the horn, and of course the "myghty bowe." It was during the fourteenth century that the English longbow (which measured about six feet) replaced the crossbow and the short bow. It became both the national weapon and the national sport, celebrated in many ballads, most of which are concerned with the feats of Robin Hood and the bowmen of Sherwood Forest. The longbow delivered an arrow some three hundred yards and it took a strong man to draw and shoot it properly, which was perhaps why bowmanship was a heroic skill in the Robin Hood stories.

Syngynge he was, or floytynge, al the day;
Singing he was, or fluting, all the day;

He was as fressh as is the month of May.
He was as fresh as is the month of May.

Short was his gowne, with sleves longe and wyde.
Short was his gown, with sleeves long and wide.

Wel koude he sitte on hors and faire ryde;
Well could he sit his horse, and fairly ride;

He koude songes make and wel endite,   95
He could make songs and compose well,

Juste and eek daunce, and wel purtreye and write.
Joust and also dance, and draw and write well.

So hote he lovede that by nyghtertale
He loved so hotly that at nighttime

He slepte namoore than dooth a nyghtyngale.
He slept no more than does a nightingale.

Curteis he was, lowely, and servysable,
Courteous he was, humble, and serviceable,

And carf biforn his fader at the table.   100
And carved before his father at the table.

    A Yeman hadde he and servantz namo
A Yeoman had he, and no other servants

At that tyme, for hym liste ride so,
At that time, for he preferred to travel so,

And he was clad in cote and hood of grene.
And he was clad in coat and hood of green.

A sheef of pecok arwes, bright and kene,
A sheaf of peacock arrows, bright and sharp,

Under his belt he bar ful thriftily;   105
Under his belt he bore right carefully;

Wel koude he dresse his takel yemanly:
Well could he handle his equipment yeomanly:

His arwes drouped noght with fetheres lowe.
His arrows didn't droop with trailing feathers.

And in his hand he bar a myghty bowe.
And in his hand he bore a mighty bow.

A not heed hadde he with a broun visage.
A cropped head had he and a brown face.

Of wodecraft wel koude he al the usage.   110
Woodcraft he understood thoroughly.

Upon his arm he bar a gay bracer,
Upon his arm he bore a gay arm guard,

And by his syde a swerd and a bokeler,
And by his side a sword and buckler,

And on that oother syde a gay daggere,
And on the other side a fine dagger,

100. "carf biforn . . .": a squire performed this function for the knight he served.

101. "Yeman": a yeoman ranked above the groom in the service of the knight, and from the description seems to have fulfilled the function of game warden.
"he": i.e., the Knight.

104. "pecock arwes": "arrows feathered with peacock feathers.

The Yeoman

21

THE PROLOGUE

[Lines 114-136]

The descriptions Chaucer has given of the Knight and his attendants are simple and straightforward, just as are they themselves. But in the presentation of the Prioress we see another kind of poetic technique, one that recurs frequently in the Prologue and the Tales. This is irony, which is a way of making apparently simple statements imply more than they actually say. This suggestive implication is a subtle way of both describing a character and commenting on him at the same time. For example, Chaucer says that the Prioress is "charitable and pitous," that is she has the virtues of charity and mercy, to be expected of someone dedicated to a religious life. The illustrations he then gives of her charity and pity concern not other people, but her pets. The "smale houndes" get (Chaucer is careful to point out) the roasted meat, milk, and finest bread that were regarded as delicacies in a society in which a good many people never had enough to eat. It seems a misdirected kind of charity and pity. Although Chaucer never tells us directly, the ironic implication throughout his portrait of the Prioress—her pretentions to aristocratic French, her fashionable manners, her dress—is that despite her holy calling she is more concerned with worldly things than with the spirit. These ironies are fairly amiable, suggesting that Chaucer likes the Prioress despite her little foibles. Later, in the treatment of the Summoner and the Pardoner, the same ironic technique is used with much more acid disapproval.

Chaucer emphasizes the Prioress' basic femininity, rather than her spiritual qualities, and he does this with a series of allusions that we miss but that a contemporary would catch immediately. These have to do with the heroines of the popular medieval romances, all of whom were described in a series of conventional phrases. Chaucer uses some of them here, such as "ful symple and coy," and he catalogues the Prioress' face (fine nose, small mouth, soft and red, fair forehead, eyes "greye as glas") in the manner of the conventional romances. There were, furthermore, several fourteenth-century romances in which the

Harneised wel and sharpe as point of spere;
Mounted well and sharp as a spear point;

A Cristophre on his brest of silver sheene.   115
A silver Christopher shone upon his breast.

An horn he bar, the bawdryk was of grene;
A horn he bore, the carrying strap was green;

A forster was he soothly, as I gesse.
He was truly a forester, as I guess.

   Ther was also a Nonne, a Prioresse,
*   There was also a Nun, a Prioress,*

That of hir smylyng was ful symple and coy.
That in her smiling was simple and sweet.

Hir gretteste ooth was but by Seint Loy;   120
Her greatest oath was but "by Saint Loy";

And she was cleped Madame Eglentyne.
And she was called Madame Eglentine.

Ful wel she soong the service dyvyne,
Full well she sang the divine service,

Entuned in hir nose ful semely;
Intoned in her nose full seemly;

And Frenssh she spak ful faire and fetisly,
And she spoke French fluently and elegantly,

After the scole of Stratford atte Bowe,   125
According to the school of Stratford-at-Bow,

For Frenssh of Parys was to hire unknowe.
For Parisian French was unknown to her.

At mete wel ytaught was she with alle:
At meals well taught was she withal:

She leet no morsel from hir lippes falle,
She let no morsel from her lips fall,

Ne wette hir fyngres in her sauce depe;
Nor wet her fingers deeply in her sauce;

Wel koude she carie a morsel, and wel kepe   130
Well could she handle a morsel, and be careful

That no drope ne fille upon hir brest.
That no drop ever fell upon her breast.

In curteisie was set ful muchel hir lest.
Courtesy was her particular interest.

Hir over-lippe wyped she so clene
Her upper lip she wiped so clean

That in hir coppe ther was no ferthyng sene
That in her cup was no trace seen

Of grece, whan she dronken hadde hir draughte;   135
Of grease, when she had drunk her draught;

Ful semely after hir mete she raughte.
Politely after her food she reached.

115. "Cristophre": the medal of St. Christopher, patron saint of foresters.

118. "Prioresse": a nun who is the superior of a priory.

The Prioress

125. "Stratford atte Bowe": about two miles outside of London, where there was the priory of St. Leonard's, with nine nuns and a prioress. While there was no real need for anyone in England to speak French in 1387, the language was probably cultivated at St. Leonard's because of its former aristocratic associations.

132. "curteisie": the Prioress' table manners were those of a lady of fashion.

THE PROLOGUE

[Lines 137-159]

heroine's name was Eglentyne. The effect, again, is an ironic association of the religious and the worldly, with the suggestion that the Prioress' real nature is closer to the second than to the first. This gives an ambiguous quality to the brooch she wears (160); supposedly the "love" of the inscription refers to the love of God but, with this particular Prioress, we suspect that it might more truly be said to refer to the love of the secular, material world.

Madame Eglentyne, as a nun, probably came from the upper levels of fourteenth-century society. This class characteristic is underlined by Chaucer in several details. Her French is not real French ("of Parys") but that of "Stratford-atte-Bowe," where the Priory of St. Leonard's was situated. The queen's sister spent many years in this priory and it had other aristocratic and courtly associations, and since French was, or had been, the language of the court it is likely that French was preserved there as a mark of social refinement. Chaucer is careful to let us know that among the pilgrims the Prioress airs her French from time to time.

And sikerly she was of greet desport,
And certainly she was very cheerful,

And ful plesaunt, and amyable of port,
And very pleasant, and amiable of disposition,

And peyned hire to countrefete cheere
And she took pains to simulate the behavior

Of court, and to been estatlich of manere,   140
Of court, and be stately in manner,

And to been holden digne of reverence.
And to be held worthy of reverence.

But for to speken of hir conscience,
But, to speak of her inner nature,

She was so charitable and so pitous
She was so charitable and full of pity

She wolde wepe if that she sawe a mous
That she would weep if she saw a mouse

Caught in a trappe, if it were deed or bledde.   145
Caught in a trap, if it were dead or bleeding.

Of smale houndes hadde she that she fedde
Some small dogs had she that she fed

With rosted flessh, or milk and wastel-breed;
With roasted meat, or milk and finest bread;

But soore wepte she if oon of hem were deed,
But sorely would she weep if one of them were dead,

Or if men smoot it with a yerde smerte;
Or if men struck it smartly with a stick;

And al was conscience and tendre herte.   150
And she was all feeling and tenderheartedness.

Ful semely hir wympel pynched was,
Most neatly her wimple was pleated,

Hir nose tretys, hir eyen greye as glas,
Her nose well shaped, her eyes gray as glass,

Hir mouth ful smal, and thereto softe and reed;
Her mouth very small, and also soft and red;

But sikerly she hadde a fair forheed;
But certainly she had a fair forehead;

It was almoost a spanne brood, I trowe,   155
It was almost a span broad, I believe,

For hardily, she was nat undergrowe.
For certainly, she was not undersized.

Ful fetys was hir cloke, as I was war;
Her cloak was very neat, I was aware;

Of smal coral aboute hir arm she bar
Of small coral about her arm she bore

A peire of bedes, gauded al with grene,
A rosary, the larger beads of green,

Pilgrim sign

151. "wympel": the wimple was a garment covering the head, sides of the face, and neck.

Man being attacked by a mob

159. "gauded": having larger, dividing beads of green.

THE PROLOGUE

[Lines 160-182]

The Second Nun

In Chaucer's representation of the Monk there is the same element of irony as in that of the Prioress. Apparently straightforward statements have critical overtones which we cannot fail to catch. Thus, after outlining in detail the Monk's extremely irreligious activities, Chaucer tells us that "Now certainly he was a fair prelaat." The inconsistency is deliberate, and we find Chaucer frequently writing in this tongue-in-cheek manner. Both the Prioress and the Monk are highly secular characters in religious institutions.

Two fundamental rules for the conduct of monks in the Middle Ages were the obligation to work and to remain within their cloister. St. Benedict's Rule (mentioned as applying to the Monk's order at 173) is clear about this: "Idleness is an enemy of the soul. Because of this brethren ought to be occupied in manual labour. . . . The monastery ought to be so constructed as to contain within it all necessaries. . . . so that there be no occasion for monks to wander abroad since this is in no wise expedient for their souls. We wish this rule to be read frequently in the community so that no brother may plead ignorance as an excuse." Chaucer's readers would of course know of this rule, and they would probably also be familiar with St. Augustine's insistence on physical labor: "the blessed Apostle Paul willed the servants of God to work corporal works which should have as their end a great spiritual reward, for this purpose that they should need food and clothing of no man, but with their own hands procure these for themselves. . . ." Chaucer notes the special exasperation that the Monk reserves for Augustine's admonition to labor. Why should he "swynken with his handes and laboure/ As Austen bit? . . . Lat Austen have his swynk to him reserved!"

Hunting is the Monk's favorite pastime and he indicates his irritation with those who objected to hunting clergy in a homely and vivid phrase—"He yaf not of that text a pulled hen/ That seith that hunters been nat holy men." Yet

And theron heng a brooch of gold ful sheene,   160
And thereon hung a brooch of brightest gold,

On which ther was first write a crowned A,
On which there was first written a crowned A,

And after *Amor vincit omnia,*
And after Amor vincit omnia.

    Another Nonne with hire hadde she,
    Another Nun with her had she,

That was hire chapeleyne and preestes thre.
Who was her chaplain, and three priests.

    A Monk ther was, a fair for the maistrie,   165
    A Monk there was, a masterful person,

An outridere that lovede venerye,
An outrider that loved hunting,

A manly man, to been an abbot able.
A manly man, capable of being an abbot.

Ful many a deyntee hors hadde he in stable,
Full many a valuable horse had he in stable,

And whan he rood, men myghte his brydel heere
And when he rode, men might his bridle hear

Gynglen in a whistlynge wynd as cleere   170
Jingling in a whistling wind as clear

And eek as loude as dooth the chapel belle.
And also as loud as the chapel bell.

Ther as this lord was kepere of the celle,
There where this lord was head of the cell,

The reule of Seint Maure or of Seint Beneit,
The rule of Saint Maur or of Saint Benedict,

By cause that it was old and somdel streit,
Because it was old and somewhat strict,

This ilke Monk leet olde thynges pace,   175
This same Monk let such old things pass,

And heeld after the newe world the space.
And followed the customs of the new world meanwhile.

He yaf nat of that text a pulled hen
He did not give a plucked hen for that text

That seith that hunters been nat holy men,
That says that hunters are not holy men,

Ne that a monk, whan he is recchelees,
Nor that a monk, when he is neglectful of rule,

Is likned til a fissh that is waterlees—   180
Is like a fish without water—

This is to seyn, a monk out of his cloystre.
That is to say, a monk without a cloister.

But thilke text heeld he nat worth an oystre;
But this text he held not worth an oyster;

The Nun's Priest

162. "Amor vincit omnia": love conquers all.

163. "Another Nonne": The Prioress naturally traveled with a companion. The chaplain was a kind of administrative assistant to the Prioress.

166. "outridere": an outrider was a monk whose duty was to oversee the monastery's estates.

173. "reule of . . .": the rules of monastic discipline established by St. Maurus and taken from St. Benedict and the Benedictine order.

The Monk

THE PROLOGUE

[Lines 183-205]

the text was a familiar one, both in St. Jerome ("Esau was a hunter and therefore a sinner") and in the writings of John Gower, a friend of Chaucer's. In his highly moral work, Mirror of Man, Gower attacks any monks who "have a horse and saddle, and money to spend.... For their pleasure these wealthy monks keep falcons and hawks for river fowl, and dogs and horses for hunting the hare...." Verbal echoes of this are plain at 189-92. Gower continues on the subject of the wealthy monk's attire: "for vain honour he is clad in a furred cloak. Let the monk be filled with consternation who makes himself handsome for the world, who wears the finest wool furred with costly grey squirrel rather than a hair shirt." Gower's "costly grey squirrel" is the trimming of the Monk's sleeves with "grys' (194), and Chaucer goes on to indicate the lavish nature of the rest of the Monk's costume, the pin "of gold yroght" which fastened his hood, the soft unwrinkled ("souple") boots, and the well-cared-for horse ("in greet estaat"). The passage concludes with one of the chief, and most expensive, delicacies of the day: roast swan.

And I seyde his opinion was good.
And I said his opinion was good.

What sholde he studie and make hymselven wood,
Why should he study and drive himself mad,

Upon a book in cloystre alwey to poure,   185
Always poring over a book in the cloister,

Or swynken with his handes and laboure,
Or work with his hands, and labor,

As Austyn bit? How shal the world be served?
As St. Augustine bids? How shall the world be served?

Lat Austyn have his swynk to him reserved!
Let St. Augustine have his work reserved for himself!

Therfore he was a prikasour aright.
Therefore he was a true huntsman.

Greyhoundes he hadde as swift as fowel in flight;   190
He had greyhounds as swift as birds in flight;

Of prikyng and of huntyng for the hare
In tracking and hunting for the hare

Wal al his lust, for no cost wolde he spare.
Was all his pleasure, for no cost would he spare.

I seigh his sleves purfiled at the hond
I saw his sleeves trimmed at the hand

With grys, and that the fyneste of a lond;
With gray fur, and that the finest in the land;

And for to festne his hood under his chyn,   195
And to fasten his hood under his chin,

He hadde of gold yroght a ful curious pyn;
He had of wrought gold an intricate pin;

A love-knotte in the gretter ende ther was.
A love knot in the large end there was.

His heed was balled, that shoon as any glas,
His head was bald, and shone like glass,

And eek his face, as he hadde been enoynt;
And also his face, as if he had been anointed;

He was a lord ful fat and in good poynt.   200
He was a lord, fat and in good condition.

His eyen stepe, and rollynge in his heed,
His eyes sharp, and rolling in his head,

That stemed as a forneys of a leed,
That glowed like a fire under a caldron,

His bootes souple, his hors in greet estaat,
His boots supple, his horse in fine shape,

Now certeinly he was a fair prelaat.
Now certainly he was a fair prelate.

He was nat pale as a forpyned goost;   205
He was not pale like a tormented ghost;

14th century costume

194. "grys": gray fur, from the squirrel, was the most expensive sort.

Ewer

THE PROLOGUE

[Lines 206-228]

Chaucer's Friar is the longest of the portraits in the Prologue, and this is perhaps because of the difficulty of the task Chaucer has set for himself. He wants to indicate the greed and hypocrisy of a certain class of fourteenth-century cleric, and also create for us an individual who is somehow likeable. Therefore he must balance the many implicit criticisms of the Friar's behavior with touches that go some way to redeeming him as a "merye" human being whose "eyen twynkled in his heed aryght/ As doon the sterres in the frosty nyght." The treatment of the Friar is mainly in terms of his social function as a member of one of the four orders of begging friars, and we must know something of the history of these orders to understand why Chaucer and other contemporary writers felt it necessary to attack them.

Friars were distinguished from monks in that their task was active service in the world as opposed to the monks' life within the cloister. There were four different orders of friars—the Franciscans, Dominicans, Carmelites, and Augustinian (or Austin) friars—all were begging orders, and all arrived in England during the thirteenth century. Though founded by different men all of the orders, in their early days, had found inspiration in the example of the founder of the Franciscans, St. Francis of Assisi. He had been Francesco Bernadone, a worldly and wealthy young man of Assisi who, early in the thirteenth century, renounced his wealth and devoted his life to religious teaching, mainly among the impoverished villages of the Italian countryside. Since he and his disciples had renounced personal wealth, St. Francis ruled that they might beg for food in times of real hardship and in this way preserve themselves to go on with their work. However the purity and zeal of the saint and his disciples did not survive long after their deaths, and by the fourteenth century the Franciscans had begun to accumulate wealth and power, as had the other begging orders. At about this time criticism of their affluence and their methods of obtaining money had begun, and Gower typifies it when he writes that "it is useless for these evil friars to plead the virtues of St. Francis when they do not follow him in any respect. Although the brethren [i.e., of the different orders] may differ from each other in dress, all are alike in their neglect of their Rule."

A fat swan loved he best of any roost.
A fat swan loved he best of any roast.

His palfrey was as broun as is a berye.
His palfrey was as brown as a berry.

A Frere ther was, a wantowne and a merye,
A Friar there was, a wanton and a merry one,

A lymytour, a ful solempne man.
A limiter, a very festive man.

In alle the ordres foure is noon that kan   210
In all the four orders there is no one that knows

So muche of daliaunce and fair langage.
So much of gossip and flattering language.

He hadde maad ful many a mariage
He had performed many a marriage

Of yonge wommen at his owene cost.
Of young women at his own cost.

Unto his ordre he was a noble post.
He was a noble pillar of his order.

Ful wel biloved and famulier was he   215
Well loved and familiar was he

With frankeleyns over al in his contree,
With rich farmers over all his country,

And eek with worthy wommen of the toun;
And also with worthy women of the town;

For he hadde power of confessioun,
For he was empowered to hear confession,

As seyde hymself, moore than a curat,
As he said himself, more than a parish priest,

For of his ordre he was licenciat.   220
For in his order he held a papal license.

Ful swetely herde he confession,
Most sweetly heard he confession,

And plesaunt was his absolucion.
And pleasant was his absolution.

He was an esy man to yeve penaunce
He was an easy man in giving penance

Ther as he wiste to have a good pitaunce;
When he knew he would have a good remuneration;

For unto a povre ordre for to yive   225
For to give to a poor order

Is signe that a man is wel yshryve;
Is a sign that a man is well shriven;

For if he yaf, he dorste make avaunt
For if one gave, he dared assert

He wiste that a man was repentaunt;
He knew that man was repentant;

207. "palfrey": saddle horse.

208. "Frere": The Friar was a member of one of the four begging orders, but Chaucer does not tell us which; these orders were often criticized in Chaucer's day. See Commentary.

209. "lymytour": one assigned a certain area in which to beg.

213. "owene cost": possibly because they had been his mistresses.

216. "frankeleyns": rich farmers, who are more fully described below, 331 ff.

218-20. i.e., he was empowered by his order to hear confessions and give absolution in cases beyond the jurisdiction of a parish priest.

The Friar

THE PROLOGUE

[Lines 229-252]

As a "lymytour" the Friar was allotted a particular geographical area in which to operate, and here again we see the way St. Francis's original notion of necessary begging had been perverted. There are two lines of the Prologue not given in our text, since they may not be genuine, but they are typical of the sort of thing being said of the friars in the period: "He yaf a certeyne ferme for the graunt/ Noon of his brethren came there in his haunt." "Ferme" is a form of rent, and the meaning is clear enough. The Friar paid for the right to beg in a district, and no other friar could beg in that area. By this time religious begging had become a remunerative occupation.

The begging friars' immorality extended beyond the monopoly of the profitable begging trade. Chaucer's Friar uses "daliaunce and fair language" to ingratiate himself with women, and if these fail there is the more concrete persuasion of "knyves and pynnes" —short, ornamental knives and brooch pins—for the "faire wyves." Scholars generally agree that the reference at 212-13 is to the friars' practice of arranging marriages for women who had been their mistresses. A fourteenth-century manuscript recounts a bishop's ruling that a priest be obliged to contribute to the upkeep of two children he had fathered on a girl, and later in The Canterbury Tales the Wife of Bath says that women need no longer fear supernatural spirits lurking under "every bussh"—their real danger is from the advances of the "lymytour."

The mendicant friars were equally corrupt in using their clerical position for gain. Late in the thirteenth century the pope had given friars permission to hear confession, and this was much abused. The friar had little interest in penitence; his purpose was to gain a "good pitaunce." We have some of Chaucer's most acid irony at 225-32, when he describes the Friar's view that all the sinner needs to do is to give money to a "poor" order to obtain divine forgiveness. The Friar knows the taverns and barmaids of every town far better than the lepers or beggars, and here again Chaucer's readers would call to mind that St. Francis had considered it one of his primary duties to look after the sick and penniless. Again, St. Francis had written that "all the brothers shall be clothed in mean garments which are to be mended with sacks and other scraps of cloth, because

For many a man so hard is of his herte,
For many a man is so hard of heart,

He may nat wepe althogh hym soore smerte. 230
He cannot weep even though he suffers sorely.

Therfore, instede of wepynge and prayeres,
Therefore, instead of weeping and prayers,

Men moote yeve silver to the povre freres.
Men should give silver to the poor friars.

His typet was ay farsed ful of knyves
His hood was always stuffed with knives

And pynnes, for to yeven faire wyves.
And pins, to give to fair women.

And certeinly he hadde a murye note; 235
And certainly he had a merry note;

Well koude he synge and pleyen on a rote;
He could sing well and play on the fiddle;

Of yeddynges he baar outrely the pris.
In songs he easily took the prize.

His nekke whit was as the flour-de-lys;
His neck was white as the lily;

Therto he strong was as a champioun.
Yet he was as strong as a champion.

He knew the tavernes wel in every toun, 240
He knew the taverns well in every town,

And every hostiler and tappestere,
And every innkeeper and barmaid,

Bet than a lazar or a beggestere.
Better than he did a leper or a female beggar.

For unto swich a worthy man as he
For such a worthy man as he

Acorded nat, as by his facultee,
It was not fitting, considering his position,

To have with sike lazars aqueyntaunce. 245
To be acquainted with sick lepers.

It is nat honeste, it may nat avaunce,
It is not worthy, it holds no profit,

For to deelen with no swich poraille,
To deal with such poor people,

But al with riche, and selleres of vitaille.
But rather with the rich, and the sellers of food.

And over al ther as profit sholde arise,
And anywhere, wherever profit might appear,

Curteis he was, and lowely of servyse; 250
He was courteous, and humble in his service;

Ther nas no man nowher so vertuous.
There was no man anywhere so virtuous.

He was the beste beggere in his hous,
He was the best beggar in his house,

233-34. "knyves and pynnes": Wycliffe attacked the friars for becoming peddlers of knives, pins, purses, etc., and for giving them to women.

236. "rote": a fiddle, or stringed instrument resembling a lyre.

238. "nekke whit": regarded in the Middle Ages as a mark of sensuality.

242. "lazar": leper (from Lazarus), but here probably any poor or diseased person.

Goblet and cover

27

THE PROLOGUE

[Lines 253-275]

God said that those who wear costly clothing belong in kingly houses." Chaucer draws attention to the richness of the Friar's dress: "lyk a maister or a pope/ Of double worstede/ was his semycope/ And rounded as a belle out of the presse." Yet despite his corruption and moral laxity, Chaucer maintains the Friar's humanity and even his likability; this is done in the last few lines, where he is associated with song and enjoyment.

Pendant

The Merchant would most probably be engaged in the export of wool and hides. Most of this trade occurred between England and the Netherlands, hence the Merchant's concern with keeping the shipping routes open between these two countries, especially since the French were said to be planning an invasion of England.

The Merchant talks "alway" of his commercial enterprises, not unlike some businessmen today. Nor is he quite as upright as he seems. The church condemned usury, or the making of money out of money ("eschaunge" being one form of this), and merchants with money to put to work were

For thogh a wydwe hadde noght a sho,
For though a widow had not even a shoe,

So plesaunt was his *In principio*
So pleasant was his In principio

Yet wolde he have a ferthyng er he wente.   255
That he would have a farthing ere he left.

His purchas was wel bettre than his rente.
His collections were larger than his income.

And rage he koude as it were right a whelpe;
And he could play as though he were a puppy;

In love-dayes ther koude he muchel helpe,
On love-days he was a great help,

For ther he was nat lyk a cloysterer
For there he was not like a cloisterer

With a thredbare cope, as is a povre scoler,   260
With threadbare cape, as is a poor scholar,

But he was lyk a maister or a pope.
But he was like a high official or a pope.

Of double worstede was his semycope,
Of double worsted was his half-cape,

And rounded as a belle out of the presse.
And rounded as the mold of a bell.

Somwhat he lipsed for his wantownesse,
He lisped a little as an affectation,

To make his Englissh sweete upon his tonge;   265
To make his English sweet upon the tongue;

And in his harpyng, whan that he hadde songe,
And in his harping, when he had sung,

His eyen twynkled in his heed aryght
His eyes twinkled in his head aright

As doon the sterres in the frosty nyght.
As do the stars in the frosty night.

This worthy lymytour was cleped Huberd.
This worthy limiter was called Hubert.

A Marchant was ther with a forked berd,   270
A Merchant was there with a forked beard,

In mottelee, and hye on horse he sat;
In motely, and high on his horse he sat;

Upon his heed a Flaundryssh bevere hat,
Upon his head a Flemish beaver hat,

His bootes clasped faire and fetisly.
His boots fastened neatly and elegantly.

His resons he spak ful solempnely,
His opinions he spoke most solemnly,

Sownynge always th'encrees of his wynnyng.   275
Proclaiming always the increase of his profits.

254. "In principio": "in the beginning [was the word]," the opening words of the Gospel of St. John and a favorite greeting among friars.

258. "love-dayes": these were days appointed for settling suits out of court.

259. "cloysterer": a poor brother who remained in the cloister.

The Merchant

270. "forked berd": in Chaucer's day, one of the fashionable ways of wearing a beard.

271. "mottelee": cloth woven with mixed colors.

THE PROLOGUE

[Lines 276-298]

forced to invent a devious sort of underground transaction ("chevyssaunce"), which was, in effect, lending money at interest. Hence the "dette" that the Merchant is in. As Mr. Rexroth has said, "The Merchant is not hoodwinking his creditors; the entire economy which the Merchant represents is founded on debt, called credit today." The Merchant is one of the first examples of the capitalist system of the financing ventures in commerce by extended loans. This sort of activity was regarded as morally delinquent. One fourteenth-century sermon says that, although God created the clergy, the knights, and the laborers, the devil created usurers, burghers, and merchants.

The Clerk of Oxenford is not quite a student in our sense of the word, but rather a member of the clergy engaged in advanced studies and one who has never been appointed to a living ("benefice"), or church post with remuneration. There is a suggestion (292) that he is not "worldly" enough to seek and gain such an appointment, and the whole description is based on this notion of dedicated, scholarly unworldliness. The Clerk is, as we would say, doing postgraduate studies. Much of this would be devoted to the works of Aristotle, who occupied a large part of the medieval university curriculum. This sort of extended scholarship was financially difficult, since the scholar had few ways of supporting himself except through gifts (299) and remuneration from the tutoring of junior students—a system already in effect in the fourteenth century and the basis for the colleges (or collection of tutoring scholars) of Oxford and Cambridge. The "twenty bookes" of Aristotle (294) means little to us today unless we recall the rarity and price of books at the time. To Chaucer's readers this library represents a tremendous financial sacrifice on the part of the Clerk.

Students are not now, and were not then, as austere as Chaucer's Clerk. Contemporary records speak of the traditional student pleasures, and gaiety, and even (at Oxford) violence. Later in The Canterbury Tales we meet Absolon, also a clerk, but perpetually engaged in music, dancing, and amorous adventures. The Clerk of the Prologue is devoted to learning, and the little he does say is

He wolde the see were kept for any thing
He wanted the sea guarded at any price

Betwixen Middelburgh and Orewelle.
Between Middleburg and Orwell.

Wel koude he in eschaunge sheeldes selle.
Well could he in bargaining sell French crowns.

This worthy man ful wel his wit besette:
This worthy man kept all his wits about him:

Ther wiste no wight that he was in dette,   280
No one knew that he was in debt,

So estatly was he of his governaunce,
So dignified was he in his dealings,

With his bargaynes, and with his chevyssaunce.
With his bargainings, and with his borrowings.

For sothe he was a worthy man with alle,
For truly he was a worthy man withal,

But, sooth to seyn, I noot how men hym calle.
But truth to tell, I do not know what he was called.

A Clerk ther was of Oxenford also,   285
A Clerk there was of Oxford also,

That unto logyk hadde longe ygo.
Who to logic had long given himself.

As leene was his hors as is a rake,
As lean was his horse as is a rake,

And he nas nat right fat, I undertake,
And he was not exactly fat, I might add,

But looked holwe, and therto sobrely.
But looked hollow-cheeked, and likewise sober.

Ful thredbare was his overeste courtepy,   290
Quite threadbare was his outer cloak,

For he hadde geten hym yet no benefice,
For he had not yet gotten himself a benefice,

Ne was so worldly for to have office.
Nor was worldly enough to seek office.

For hym was levere have at his beddes heed
For he would rather have at his bed's head

Twenty bookes, clad in blak or reed,
Twenty books, bound in black and red,

Of Aristotle and his philosophie,   295
Of Aristotle and his philosophy,

Than robes riche, or fithele, or gay sautrie.
Than rich robes, or a fiddle, or a gay harp.

But al be that he was a philosophre,
But although he was a philosopher,

Yet hadde he but litel gold in cofre;
Yet had he little gold in his coffer;

The Clerk of Oxenford

277. Middelburgh was a port in the low countries, and Orwell a river in Suffolk.

278. This foreign exchange of currency was illegal.

285. "Clerk": at Oxford, an ecclesiastical student.

286. i.e., he had studied logic, which was part of his qualification for the B.A.

291. "benefice": appointment to the rectorship of a parish church.

294. "Twenty bookes": a large library at this time.

297. "philosophre": the word also meant alchemist, and this is a pun on that second meaning.

THE PROLOGUE

[Lines 299-321]

"sownynge in moral vertu." Physically he is austere. His horse is lean as a rake, "And he was nat right fat, I undertake." We think, by contrast, of the fat Monk and his well-fed mount, as Chaucer intends us to. There is no question of irony or satire in the description of the Clerk. Chaucer respects him without qualification and has given to him the simplest, finest, and briefest eulogy that any scholar-teacher has ever had: "And gladly wolde he lerne and gladly teche."

Do not confuse the term "Sergeant" as Chaucer uses it here with modern noncommissioned military rank. In the fourteenth century it designated a special order of barristers, or lawyers, who were selected by the reigning monarch and from whose ranks the common law judges were chosen until 1890, when the order was abolished. The sergeants of the law were on the same social level as knights and the sons of noblemen. In Chaucer's time there were only about two dozen of them in the whole of England.

Chaucer does not question his lawyer's ability, or his knowledge of the law. Since English law is largely "case law," in which precedents direct particular judgments, a lawyer's knowledge of previous decisions must be extensive. Yet the statement that the lawyer knows all the "doomes" (judgments) since William the Conqueror is another example of Chaucer's deliberate exaggeration —we are to infer that he talked as though he knew them all. Chaucer's attitude toward the lawyer becomes explicit at 321-22, and here again the criticism is universally valid; we still have with us those who are anxious to give the impression that they are constantly involved in matters of great import, who "seem busier than they are."

Chaucer subtly suggests the lawyer's failings. He is "war and wys," but it is his cunning, not his goodness, that is emphasized. He

But al that he myghte of his freendes hente,
But all that he might get from his friends,

On bookes and on lernynge he it spente,　　300
On books and learning he spent,

And bisily gan for the soules preye
And busily prayed for the souls

Of hem that yaf him wherwith to scoleye.
Of those that gave him wherewithal to study.

Of studie took he moost cure and moost heede.
Of study took he most care and most heed.

Noght o word spak he moore than was neede,
Not a word did he speak more than was needed,

And that was seyd in forme and reverence,　　305
And that was said with propriety and modesty,

And short and quyk, and ful of hy sentence;
And brief and lively, and full of high meaning;

Sownynge in moral vertu was his speche,
Concerned with moral virtue was his speech,

And gladly wolde he lerne and gladly teche.
And gladly would he learn and gladly teach.

A Sergeant of the Lawe, war and wys,
A Sergeant-of-Law, wary and wise,

That often hadde been at the Parvys,　　310
Who often had been at the church porch,

Ther was also, ful riche of excellence.
There was also, rich in excellence.

Discreet he was, and of greet reverence—
Discreet he was, and of great reverence—

He semed swich, his wordes weren so wise.
He seemed so, his words were so wise.

Justice he was ful often in assise,
A justice was he often in assize,

By patente and by pleyn commissioun.　　315
By patent and by full commission.

For his science and for his heigh renoun
For his knowledge and for his high renown

Of fees and robes hadde he many oon.
Of fees and robes had he many a one.

So greet a purchasour was nowher noon;
So great a buyer of land was nowhere known;

Al was fee symple to hym in effect;
All was fee simple to him in effect;

His purchasyng myghte nat been infect.　　320
His purchases could not be contested.

Nowher so bisy a man as he ther nas,
There was nowhere so busy a man as he,

The Sergeant-At-Law

309. "Sergeant": a lawyer of the highest degree, chosen from the most eminent senior members of the bar.

310. "Parvys": this was the porch of St. Paul's cathedral, a favorite place for lawyers to congregate, and perhaps meet clients.

314. "assise": the regular county court.

315. "patente": letter of appointment from the king.
"commissioun": commissioned to hear cases of all sorts.

319. "fee symple": a title of ownership without restriction.

THE PROLOGUE

is rich (a great "purchasour"), but this is through sharp legal practice. Many of Chaucer's contemporaries denounced lawyers for promoting legal conflicts, bribing those who gave evidence and using the law to get control of lands. Langland in Piers Plowman attacked the cupidity of lawyers, saying that it was "easier to measure the mist on the Malvern Hills" than to get an opinion from a lawyer until he had been paid.

It is significant that the Sergeant of Law should be traveling in the company of the Franklin. The lawyer would choose no ordinary member of society as his companion and the Franklin, as Chaucer makes very clear, was a substantial person in every way. He presided at sessions of justices of the peace (355), had been a member of parliament (356, the "knyght" was the representative of the "shire"), and had been a sheriff and a treasurer (359).

One of the first things we learn about the Franklin is that "Of his complexion he was sangwyn," a phrase which carried a much more elaborate meaning to the fourteenth-century reader than it does to us.

Medieval medical science classified people according to the "humour," or fluid, which was dominant in them. Thus the humors were supposed to control and determine the character. This doctrine of humors was based on the belief that all matter could be reduced to four elements; air, fire, water, and earth. In the body these were the four fluids: blood, yellow bile, phlegm, and black bile. A person's quality or temperament depended upon the way these fluids, or humors, were mixed in him. Thus a dominance of black bile, which corresponds to earth, made a man dull and melancholic.

The word sanguine is derived from the word blood, and the Franklin's character was dominated by the humor of blood. This was understood to produce several qualities—generosity,

And yet he semed bisier than he was.
And yet he seemed busier than he was.

In terms hadde he caas and doomes alle
He could recite all the cases and judgments,

That from the tyme of kyng William were falle.
That had taken place from the time of King William.

Thereto he koude endite and make a thyng,   325
He could so draw up and make a document,

Ther koude no wight pynche at his writyng;
That no man could find a flaw in his writing;

And every statut koude he pleyn by rote.
And every statute he could recite by rote.

He rood but hoomly in a medlee cote,
He rode unpretentiously in a motley coat,

Girt with a ceint of silk with barres smale.
Belted with a girdle of silk with small stripes.

Of his array telle I no lenger tale.   330
Of his dress I tell no longer tale.

A Frankeleyn was in his compaignye;
A Franklin was in his company;

Whit was his berd as is the dayesye;
White was his beard as is the daisy;

Of his complexion he was sangwyn.
Of a ruddy complexion.

Wel loved he by the morwe a sop in wyn;
Well loved he in the morning a sop of wine;

To lyven in delit was evere his wone,   335
To live pleasurably was ever his custom,

For he was Epicurus owene sone,
For he was Epicurus' own son,

That heeld opinion that pleyn delit
Who held the theory that complete delight

Was verraily felicitee parfit.
Was truly the perfect felicity.

An housholdere, and that a greet, was he;
A householder, and a great one, was he;

Saint Julian he was in his contree.   340
Saint Julian he was in his country.

His breed, his ale, was alwey after oon;
His bread, his ale were always equally good;

A bettre envyned man was nowher noon.
A man with a better wine cellar did not exist.

Withoute bake mete was nevere his hous,
His house was never without meat pie,

Of fissh and flessh, and that so plentevous,
Of fish and flesh, and that so plenteous,

The Franklin

331. "Frankeleyn": a well-to-do landholder.

336. The philosophy of Epicurus was held to recommend luxurious living.

340. "Saint Julian": patron saint of hospitality.

THE PROLOGUE

[Lines 345-367]

kindness, a large appetite, and pleasure in physical satisfaction in general. So the word "sangwyn," which to us simply means of a reddish complexion, contained a whole character analysis for Chaucer's readers, and the account of the Franklin is simply an elaboration of that character.

Much of the elaboration has to do with the Franklin's love for food and the amplitude of his larder ("It snewed in his hous of mete and drynke.") His breakfast (334) is typical. The "sop of wyn" that he takes was more than simply a piece of bread dipped in wine; it was a rich glazed dish, made by pouring a sauce of wine, almond milk, saffron, ginger, sugar, cinnamon, cloves, and mace over a loaf of the best white bread.

One fifteenth-century book gives the menu for a "Fest for a franklen." The guests were to be served a first course of "brawn with mustard, bacon and peas; beef and boiled chickens, roast goose, capon and custard, a dish of pastries stuffed with a mixture of cream, eggs, marrow, prunes, dates and spices. The second course consists of a rich stew made of meat or fish, veal, lamb, kid, or rabbit, chickens or pigeons roasted, little pastries stuffed with cream, eggs, spices and meats; thin slices of fried bread and apples or pears when in season; bread and cheese, spiced cakes and wafers, with a drink which was a mixture of ale, honey and spices" (Bowden).

Chaucer's five guildsmen come from different crafts yet wear the same uniform, so that they must belong to a parish rather than a craft guild. When we think of the medieval guild system we usually think of the craft guilds—associations of people who are all in the same trade, such as the fishermen's guild or the silversmith's guild, but there were also guilds formed geographically, by parish, especially in London. These originated in the practicing members of a parish joining together to support a priest to perform various religious functions for them, but they soon developed into powerful associations with many other functions, at first social and benevolent, and later political. The guilds held feasts, collected dues, tried quarrels between their members, helped those in trouble, and

It snewed in his hous of mete and drynke, 345
It snowed in his house of meat and drink,

Of alle deyntees that men koude thynke.
Of all dainties that one could think of.

After the sondry sesons the yeer,
According to the various seasons of the year,

So chaunged he his mete and his soper.
He varied his meat and his supper.

Ful many a fat partrich hadde he in muwe,
Full many a fat partridge had he in coop,

And many a breem and many a luce in stuwe. 350
And many a bream and many a pike in his pond.

Wo was his cook but if his sauce were
Woe to his cook, unless his sauces were

Poynaunt and sharp, and redy al his geere.
Pungent and sharp, and all his equipment ready.

His table dormant in his halle alway
His table stationed in his hall always

Stood redy covered al the longe day.
Stood ready set all the day long.

At sessions ther was he lord and sire; 355
At court sessions was he lord and sire;

Ful ofte tyme he was knyght of the shire.
Often he was knight of the shire.

An anlaas and a gipser al of silk
A dagger and a pouch of silk

Heeng at his girdel, whit as morne milk.
Hung at his girdle, white as morning milk.

A shirreve hadde he been, and a countour.
A sheriff had he been, and a treasurer.

Was nowher swich a worthy vavasour. 360
There was nowhere such a worthy vassal.

An Haberdasshere and a Carpenter,
A Haberdasher and a Carpenter,

A Webbe, a Dyere, and a Tapycer—
A Weaver, a Dyer, and an Upholsterer—

And they were clothed alle in o lyveree
Were with us too, clothed in one livery

Of a solempne and a greet fraternitee.
Of a distinguished and great guild.

Ful fressh and newe hir geere apiked was; 365
Full fresh and new their clothes were trimmed;

Hir knyves were chaped noght with bras,
Their knives were mounted not with brass,

But al with silver; wroght ful clene and weel
But all with silver; wrought full clean and well

Covered cup

356. "knyght of the shire": the representative of the county in parliament.

361. "Haberdasshere": a seller of hats, needles, buttons, etc.

362. "Tapycer": upholsterer or tapestry maker.

364. One of the parish guilds, a religious and fraternal organization.

THE PROLOGUE

[Lines 368-390]

expelled those who broke their rules. Their political power, by the fourteenth century, usually took the form of throwing their support (which was considerable) either on the side of parliament against the king, or vice versa. They were an important social force, and certainly "a solempne and greet fraternitee."

Chaucer tells us that each of his guildsmen seemed "a fair burgeys," able to sit on the dais of a guildhall. Since only the mayor and aldermen were allowed to do this, Chaucer probably means only to imply that each of them was worthy of the rank of alderman, "for the wisdom that he kan." Certainly their wives thought they were (374). In a sly aside (375-78), Chaucer touches on that wifely trait which is a universal rather than a specifically medieval thing. The suggestion is that the ambition to be alderman on the part of his characters is inspired in a large part by their wives' desire to be styled "lady" or "madame" and head the procession at the "vigilies."

The guildsmen are at least substantial enough to be able to bring their own cook with them on the pilgrimage to Canterbury. Brief though it is, the account makes him an individual, a competent cook with a "mormal" on his shin who could "knowe a draught of London ale." According to the physicians of the day, the ulcerous "mormal" was the direct result of "the eating of melancholic foods and the drinking of strong wines."

The Shipman

The Shipman—the master of the Madelaine—represents an occupation rapidly gaining in importance in Chaucer's day. Seagoing activities were increasing and from the fourteenth century on, the sea and those who sailed on it, would be vital to England's interests. The Shipman is pre-

---

Hire girdles and hir pouches everydeel.
Their girdles and their pouches were in keeping.

Wel semed ech of hem a fair burgeys
Each of them seemed a sufficiently good citizen

To sitten in a yeldehalle on a deys.   370
To sit in a guildhall on a dais.

Everich, for the wisdom that he kan,
Each, for the knowledge that he had,

Was shaply for to been an alderman.
Was fit to be an alderman.

For catel hadde they ynogh and rente,
For property had they enough and income,

And eek hir wyves wolde it wel assente—
And also their wives would agree to it—

And elles certeyn were they to blame.   375
And otherwise certainly they would be to blame.

It is ful fair to been ycleped "Madame,"
It is indeed pleasant to be called "Madam,"

And goon to vigilies al bifore,
And go to vigils before everyone,

And have a mantel roialliche ybore.
And have a mantle royally carried.

A Cook they hadde with hem for the nones,
A Cook they had with them for the occasion,

To boille the chiknes with the marybones,   380
To boil the chickens with the marrow bones,

And powdre-marchant tart and galyngale.
And tart flavoring and spice.

Wel koude he knowe a draughte of London ale.
Well could he appreciate a draught of London ale.

He koude rooste and sethe and broille and frye,
He could roast and boil and broil and fry,

Maken mortreux, and wel bake a pye.
Make a stew, and well bake a pie.

But greet harm was it, as it thoughte me,   385
But a great pity was it, as I thought,

That on his shyne a mormal hadde he.
That on his shin he had an ulcer.

For blankmanger, that made he with the beste.
As for spiced chicken, he made that with the best.

A Shipman was ther, wonynge fer by weste;
A Sailor was there, living to the west;

For aught I woot, he was of Dertemouthe.
For all I know, he was from Dartmouth.

He rood upon a rouncy as he kouthe,   390
He rode upon a large horse as well as he could,

---

370. The dais was reserved for the mayor and aldermen.

376. The wives of aldermen assumed the title "lady."

377. "vigilies": ceremonial processions on the eve of festivals; the aldermen's wives headed the procession.

The Cook

389. "Dertemouthe": Dartmouth in the southwest was a large port in the Middle Ages.

THE PROLOGUE

[Lines 391-413]

sented as a rough-and-ready character ("Of nyce conscience took he no keep") as anyone in his position was obliged to be. The seas were the scene of a good deal of international piracy. There was as yet, in England, only a small national maritime force—"the King's ships," as they were called—and therefore the individual merchantmen traveled armed, ready either to repel attack or, on occasion, to initiate it. The men of the west country ports, such as Dartmouth, had been issued what amounted to a royal license for privateering against England's seagoing enemies, in part to protect English trade, in part to enrich themselves.

The Shipman is immediately identified by his inability to ride; the phrase "as he kouthe" (390) might be more fully translated as "insofar as he was able to do it at all." We must also suppose that "certeinly he was a good felawe" (395) is in some degree ironic, since it is immediately followed by an account of the way in which the Shipman steals wine from the "chapman," or merchant, who was paying him to convey and protect it. Contemporary documents indicate a good deal of irritation at the French and English wine merchants, who frequently delivered casks of wine incompletely filled. Chaucer seems here to be suggesting that the fault may not always lie with the merchant. The Shipman's easy conscience extends to more than wine-stealing. When victor in combat at sea, he unburdens himself of his prisoners by making them walk the plank—"By water he sente them hoom to every lond." This was the accepted practice of the day. When King Edward won a naval victory over the Spaniards and captured one of their vessels (in 1350), he threw all its crew overboard, and this was regarded as the appropriate thing for a victor to do.

Despite the confused and sometimes superstitious state of medical theory in the Middle Ages, anyone entering the practice had a good deal of study before him, as we can see from Chaucer's list of authorities known to his "Doctour of Physik." A great deal had been written about the functioning of the human body, most of it,

In a gowne of faldyng to the knee.
In a gown of coarse cloth to the knee.

A daggere hangynge on a laas hadde he
A dagger hanging on a cord had he

Aboute his necke, under his arms adoun.
Around his neck and beneath his arm.

The hoote somer hadde maad his hewe al broun;
The hot summer had made his color brown;

And certeinly he was a good felawe.   395
And certainly he was a good fellow.

Ful many a draughte of wyn hadde he ydrawe
Full many a draught of wine had he drawn

Fro Burdeux-ward, whil that the chapman sleep;
Coming from Bordeaux, while the merchant slept;

Of nyce conscience took he no keep.
Of scrupulous conscience he took no heed.

If that he faught and hadde the hyer hond,
If he fought and gained the upper hand,

By water he sente hem hoom to every lond.   400
By water he sent them home to every land.

But of his craft, to rekene wel his tydes,
But as to his skill in reckoning his tides,

His stremes and his daungers hym bisides,
His currents and his other dangers besides,

His herberwe and his moone, his lodemenage,
His harbor and his moon, his pilotage,

Ther nas noon swich from Hulle to Cartage.
There was none such from Hull to Carthage.

Hardy he was and wys to undertake;   405
Hardy he was and shrewd in his ventures;

With many a tempest hadde his berd been shake;
By many a tempest had his beard been shaken;

He knew alle the havenes as they were,
He knew all the harbors as they were,

Fro Gootlond to the Cape of Fynystere,
From Gotland to the Cape of Finisterre,

And every cryke in Britaigne and in Spayne.
And every creek in Brittany and Spain.

His barge ycleped was the Maudelayne.   410
His ship was called the Madelaine.

With us ther was a Doctour of Phisik;
With us there was a Doctor of Medicine;

In al this world ne was ther noon hym lik,
In all this world there never was his like,

To speke of phisik and surgerye,
To speak of medicine and surgery,

395. "good felawe": the expression was sometimes used ironically, for "rascal," which seems to be the intention here.

The Doctor of Physic

404. "Hulle to Cartage": Hull, in Yorkshire, and probably Cartagena, in Spain, rather than Carthage.

408. "Gootlond": an island in the Baltic near Sweden. Fynystere; on the west coast of Spain.

THE PROLOGUE

[Lines 414-436]

from our point of view, wildly unscientific. Medical knowledge was a combination of what had been inherited from the ancients—Hippocrates and Galen—some Mohammedan lore, and a good deal of folk knowledge of botanical and herbal cures. However, the degree of Doctor of Physic took as long to get in the fourteenth century as it does today, and the learning involved is retailed by Chaucer at 429-34. Esculapius is the legendary father of medicine. "Olde Ypocras is Hippocrates, a Greek of the fifth century B.C. Deiscorides, a Roman, was the author of what was probably the most important work of pharmacology in the ancient world and Rufus was an anatomist. Galen (regarded by the Middle Ages as the principal ancient authority) flourished in 200 A.D., and was largely responsible for the physiological theory of "humours," which Chaucer's doctor would, of course, accept. There follows (432) a series of Moslem authorities, attesting to the high regard in which Moslem medical theory was held at the time and also, incidentally, pointing to one of the reasons the medieval people suspected their doctors of lacking Christian belief (438): they had been exposed to too much Moslem writing. Gilbertyn (Gilbertus Angelicus), of the thirteenth century, was an English physician with a European reputation. What remains of his writings shows some remarkably advanced theories for the period. He pointed out the contagious nature of smallpox, said that cancer could only be cured by surgery, and outlined a diet which is very like the vitamin-balanced diets of today. Gatesden was physician to Edward II, and became a great favorite by curing one of the princes of smallpox (which he did by "wrapping him in scarlet cloths").

For the theory of humors alluded to at 421 the reader is referred back to the commentary on the "sangwyn" Franklin at 333. Chaucer also draws attention to the fact the learned doctor was "grounded in astronomye." This is, of course, what we call astrology—the study of the influence of the stars on human affairs and especially the individual's health.

Here is John Livingston Lowes' account of the use of "astronomye": "To Chaucer's contemporary readers the necessity of a physician's expert knowledge of astronomy was as obvious as to us the indispensability of a surgeon's grounding in anatomy. For the doctor's remedies had to be administered at the proper planetary hours. And those were the hours at which the constitution of the patient and the constitution of a

For he was grounded in astronomye.
For he was grounded in astrology.

He kepte his pacient a ful greet deel   415
He cared for his patient very carefully

In houres by his magyk natureel.
According to the stars, by his natural magic.

Wel koude he fortunen the ascendent
Well could he understand the fortunes of the rise

Of his ymages for his pacient.
Of the signs pertaining to his patient.

He knew the cause of every maladye,
He knew the cause of every sickness,

Were it of hoot or cold or moyste or drye,   420
Whether of hot or cold or moist or dry,

And were engendred and of what humour;
And where engendered and of which humor;

He was a verray, parfit praktisour.
He was a very perfect practitioner.

The cause yknowe, and of his harm the roote,
The cause known, and of his disease the root,

Anon he yaf the sike man his boote.
At once he gave the sick man his remedy.

Ful redy hadde he his apothecaries   425
All ready had he his apothecaries

To sende him drogges and his letuaries,
To send him his drugs and medicines,

For ech of hem made oother for to wynne;
For each of them made profit for the other;

Hir frendshipe nas nat newe to bigynne.
Their friendship had not just begun.

Wel knew he the olde Esculapius,
Well did he know the old Aesculapias,

And Deiscorides and eek Rufus,   430
And Dioscorides, and also Rufus,

Olde Ypocras, Haly, and Galyen,
Old Hippocrates, Haly and Galen,

Serapion, Razis, and Avycen,
Serapion, Rhasis, and Avicenna,

Averrois, Damascien, and Constantyn,
Averroes, Damascene, and Constantine,

Bernard and Gatesden and Gilbertyn.
Bernard and Gatisden and Gilbertine.

Of his diete mesurable was he,   435
In his diet he was moderate,

For it was of no superfluitee,
For it had no superfluity,

414. "astronomye": the influence of the stars, our astrology, was considered most important in the practice of medicine.

420. These were the qualities, or "humours"—also called the sanguine, phlegmatic, choleric, and melancholy—the proper balance of which in the body was necessary to health.

429-34. The men here mentioned were the authors of the chief medical textbooks of the Middle Ages.

Seal of the Uppingham school

THE PROLOGUE

[Lines 437-458]

sign or planet were in due correspondence. For human beings were compounded of the four elements in definite admixtures—hot and moist, hot and dry, cold and moist, cold and dry. But so were likewise constituted the planets and the zodiacal signs—Mars hot and dry, Venus hot and moist, Taurus cold and dry, and so on. And the eternal movement of seven variously constituted planets through twelve diversely constituted signs was bound at some moment to bring about in the heavens a conjunction of elements which stood in such relation to their maladjusted mixture in the patient as would render the application of the proper remedy effective. And it was expert knowledge of the intricate relations between the elemental characters of planets, signs, and sick men taken together which the medieval doctor had to have. His 'natural magic' was precisely that recondite skill."

The Wife of Bath is one of Chaucer's most famous characters. He makes her a vivid presence here in the Prologue, and enlarges the portrait later in The Canterbury Tales in her own prologue to her own tale. The geographical notation "biside Bathe" is not as vague as it sounds. It meant the small parish just outside the north gate of Bath called "St. Michael-without-the-walls," and it was probably at the door of St. Michael's church that the Wife's many marital encounters took place.

The Wife's great talent is for cloth-making, and we get Chaucer's tongue-in-cheek touch again when he asserts her superiority over the cloth-makers "of Ypres and of Gaunt," an opinion that we suspect came straight from the Wife herself. There follows an illuminating little touch concerning her character. No woman in the parish, Chaucer says, ought to precede the Wife to the "offrynge" in church. And if any did "certeyn so wrooth was she/ That she was out of alle charitee." We can well imagine it, and so the tone is set for the development of this boisterous, egotistical, but fundamentally very likeable character later in the Tales.

Here two points are made about the Wife: her amorous nature and her habit of going on pilgrimages. The reference to the husbands "at chirche dore" is explained by the fact that medieval marriages were performed at the entrance of the church, since most of the service was not in Latin, the wedding group proceeding inside afterward for the nuptial mass. But the striking thing about the line is the number of mates the Wife has had. In part the reason

But of greet norissyng and digestible.
But was greatly nourishing and digestible.

His studie was but litel on the Bible.
His study was but little of the Bible.

In sangwyn and in pers he clad was al,
In blood-red and blue-gray he was clad,

Lyned with taffata and with sendal;   440
Lined with taffeta and fine silk;

And yet he was but esy of dispence;
And yet he was slow in spending;

He kepte that he wan in pestilence.
He kept what he earned during the plague;

For gold in phisik is a cordial,
For gold in medicine is a cordial,

Therfore he loved gold in special.
Therefore he loved gold especially.

A good Wif was ther of biside Bathe,   445
  A good Wife was there from near Bath,

But she was somdel deef, and that was scathe.
But she was somewhat deaf, and that was a pity.

Of clooth-makyng she hadde swich an haunt,
Of cloth-making she had such a knack,

She passed hem of Ypres and of Gaunt.
She surpassed them of Ypres and Ghent.

In al the parisshe wif ne was ther noon
In all the parish, woman was there none

That to the offrynge bifore hire sholde goon;   450
That to the collection box before her should go;

And if ther dide, certeyn so wrooth was she,
And if any did, certainly so angry was she,

That she was out of alle charitee.
That she lost all charity.

Hir coverchiefs ful fyne were of ground;
Her kerchiefs were finely woven;

I dorste swere they weyeden ten pound
I dare swear they weighed ten pounds

That on a Sonday weren upon hir heed.   455
That on a Sunday were upon her head.

Hir hosen weren of fyn scarlet reed,
Her hose were of fine scarlet red,

Ful streite yteyd, and shoes ful moyste and newe.
Tightly tied, and shoes all soft and new.

Boold was hir face and fair and reed of hewe.
Bold was her face, and fair, and red of hue.

438. Physicians were held to be skeptics.

Wife of Bath.

448. Ypres and Gaunt were Flemish towns noted for their fine fabrics.

450. The parishioners came forward in order of rank.

Widow's barbe and veil

THE PROLOGUE

[Lines 459–482]

is economic—the Wife is a woman of property and the possessor of a commercially valuable skill. The Middle Ages were more romantic in their literature than in life, and just as a dowerless woman found it difficult to get married, so one with money found it easy. But the main reason for the many marriages is simply that the Wife enjoyed the company of men. Chaucer goes on to suggest the "oother compaignye in youthe," but gallantly refuses, in the next line (462), to elaborate on the Wife's premarital liaisons. How would a woman of the Wife's ebullient and garrulous nature ("wel koude she laughe and carpe") get on in marriage? Here we are told that she is "somdel deef," but later in the *Tales* we discover that this is because her fifth husband once became so infuriated with her that he beat her about the head and impaired her hearing.

There is no real inconsistency in a woman of the Wife's worldly nature going on a series of pilgrimages to holy shrines. By the fourteenth century the pilgrimage had become for some a social excursion as well as a religious act, a fact reflected in some of Chaucer's other less-than-devout pilgrims. Some of the contemporary writers complain of married women going on pilgrimages, and it may well have been a device for escaping the restrictions imposed by a husband. Jerusalem was, of course, the principal destination for pilgrimages. The Wife has been there three times, where she would have been shown the white stone on which the True Cross stood, and near which the first crusaders were buried. She has also been to Rome, where the major pilgrim attractions were St. Peter's (a visit there procuring many years of pardon), and St. Paul's Cathedral, where the stone on which St. Paul was beheaded was said to cure the sick and maimed who touched it.

Most of the figures in The Canterbury Tales (and in the tales they tell) have the normal portion of human failings and some of them a good deal more than the normal, but the Parson is a study in virtue. One of the reasons for this lies in the other clerics—notably the Pardoner and the Summoner—who are thoroughly corrupt. It was Chaucer's intention to delineate the failings of individual people, not the institution they happened to be part of, and in the creation of the good Parson he tells us by implication that the church does have servants who faithfully carry out its commands.

She was a worthy womman al hir lyve:
She was a worthy woman all her life:

Housbondes at chirche dore she hadde fyve,   460
Husbands at church door she had five,

Withouten oother compaignye in youthe—
Not to mention other companions in youth—

But therof nedeth nat to speke as nowthe.
But there is no need to discuss that now.

And thries hadde she been at Jerusalem;
And thrice had she been at Jerusalem;

She hadde passed many a straunge strem;
She had crossed many a foreign stream;

At Rome she hadde been, and at Boloigne,   465
At Rome she had been, and at Boulogne,

In Galice at Seint Jame, and at Coloigne;
In Galicia at Saint James, and at Cologne;

She koude muche of wandrynge by the weye.
She knew much of wayfaring.

Gat-tothed was she, soothly for to seye.
Gap-toothed was she, to tell the truth.

Upon an amblere esily she sat,
Upon an ambling horse easily she sat,

Ywympled wel, and on hir heed an hat   470
Neatly veiled, and on her head a hat

As brood as is a bokeler or a targe;
As wide as a buckler or a shield;

A foot-mantel aboute hir hipes large,
An outer skirt about her large hips,

And on hir feet a paire of spores sharpe.
And on her feet a pair of sharp spurs.

In felaweshipe wel koude she laughe and carpe.
In company well could she laugh and joke.

Of remedies of love she knew per chaunce,   475
She doubtless knew the remedies of love,

For she koude of that art the olde daunce.
For she knew that art from of old.

A good man was ther of religioun,
A good man there was of religion,

And was a povre Person of a toun,
Who was a poor Parson of a town,

But riche he was of holy thoght and werk.
But he was rich in holy thought and work.

He was also a lerned man, a clerk,   480
He was also a learned man, a clerk,

That Cristes gospel trewely wolde preche;
That Christ's gospel would truly preach;

His parisshens devoutly wolde he teche.
And parishioners would he devoutly teach.

460. In the Middle Ages marriages were performed at the church door.

463. "Jerusalem": pronounced as three distinct syllables.

465-66. As well as the Holy Sepulcher at Jerusalem, the Wife of Bath had visited the other famous shrines at Rome, Boulogne, St. James of Compostella in Galicia, and Cologne.

475. "remedies of love": the phrase was associated with the Latin poet Ovid's Remedia Amoris.

The poor Parson

THE PROLOGUE

[Lines 483-506]

The Parson is in some ways a parallel to the Knight, the latter exhibiting virtue in the secular world as the former does in the ecclesiastical. One effect of this somewhat special treatment is to make the Parson a little less solid as a character than the other pilgrims. Since Chaucer is mainly concerned with the Parson's virtuous qualities, he does not provide those sharply observed details of appearance or habits of speech and action that render the others so vividly.

One abuse which was rife in the Middle Ages among clerics is implied by the Parson's refusal to "cursen"—that is, to excommunicate—those who did not pay their tithes. For the members of a parish this tenth part of their wealth was a heavy imposition, yet the punishment for not paying it was excommunication, which was a very real and terrifying fate. The representatives of the church had a powerful hold over the people, and we shall see later how some of them abused it. Chaucer's Parson not only does not use this threat, but aids his parishoners from the general "offryng," or collection, and even from his own "substaunce."

14th century costume

Benygne he was and wonder diligent,
Benign he was, and wonderfully diligent,

And in adversitee ful pacient;
And in adversity entirely patient;

And swich he was ypreved ofte sithes.   485
And so he had proved many times.

Ful looth were hym to cursen for his tithes,
Altogether loath was he to excommunicate for his tithes,

But rather wolde he yeven, out of doute,
But rather would he give, without a doubt,

Unto his povre parisshens aboute
To his various poor parishioners

Of his offryng and eek of his substaunce;
Of his collection, and also of his own income;

He koude in litel thyng have suffisaunce.   490
He could with little have sufficient.

Wyd was his parisshe, and houses fer asonder,
Wide was his parish, and houses far apart,

But he ne lefte nat for reyn ne thonder,
But he did not neglect for rain or thunder,

In siknesse nor in meschief, to visite
In sickness or in trouble, to visit

The ferreste in his parisshe, muche and lite,
The farthest in his parish, great and small,

Upon his feet, and in his hand a staf.   495
On foot, with a staff in his hand.

This noble ensample to his sheep he yaf
This noble example to his sheep he gave

That first he wroghte, and afterward he taughte.
That first he practiced, and afterward he preached.

Out of the gospel he tho wordes caughte,
Out of the gospel he took those words,

And this figure he added eek therto:
And this figure of speech he added to it:

That if gold ruste, what shal iren do?   500
That if gold rust, what shall iron do?

For if a preest be foul, on whom we truste,
For if a priest be foul, in whom we trust,

No wonder is a lewed man to ruste.
No wonder that an unlearned man will rust.

And shame it is, if a preest take keep:
And shameful it is, let priests take note,

A shiten shepherde and a clene sheep.
A befouled shepherd and a clean sheep.

Wel oghte a preest ensample for to yive   505
Well ought a priest to set an example,

By his clennesse how that his sheep sholde lyve.
By his cleanliness, how his sheep should live.

486. Excommunicate in order to force payment of tithes.

489. "substaunce": his own income, derived from his benefice and from tithes.

497. i.e., he practiced what he preached.

500. i.e., if the highest should weaken, what would the lowest do?

THE PROLOGUE

[Lines 507-530]

The major virtue that Chaucer attributes to his Parson is that he practices what he preaches: "first he wroghte, and afterward he taughte." The members of any religious hierarchy are always especially vulnerable to the charge that there is a discrepancy between what they teach and what they themselves do. The obligation to be a moral leader puts them in a special position, which Chaucer sums up in a line which has become part of the language's store of proverbs: "That if gold ruste, what shal iren do?" Another contemporary abuse is glanced at in the next passage (507-12). This is clerical absenteeism, which usually took the form of serving in one of the especially endowed chantries in the city (many of which were set up by the guilds) while simply abandoning the rural parish, or hiring a substitute. This had the advantages of increasing the cleric's finances, since the city chantries and foundations were usually wealthy, and also of avoiding the rigorous life of the country parish.

There are some scholars who believe that Chaucer's Parson is meant to be a representative of that group of fourteenth-century religious reformers who were followers of John Wycliffe (1320-84). They were called Lollards (the name was supposed to represent the mumbling delivery of their sermons), and they attacked the church's wealth and advocated the poverty of the clergy. The Parson himself never supports these arguments, but probably Chaucer agreed with some of the Lollard views.

Goblet

The Plowman is the Parson's brother, and the connection is made deliberately, since they both represent the virtues of their respective occupations. Chaucer probably does not here reflect the

He sette nat his benefice to hyre,
He did not hire out his benefice,

And leet his sheep encombred in the myre,
And leave his sheep sunk in the mire,

And ran to London, unto Seinte Poules,
And run to London, to Saint Paul's,

To seken hym a chaunterie for soules,   510
To apply for a place as a chanter for souls,

Or with a bretherhede to been withholde;
Or to be retained by a guild;

But dwelte at hoom and kepte wel his folde,
But lived at home, and guarded well his fold,

So that the wolf ne made it nat myscarie;
So that the wolf would do it no harm;

He was a shepherde and noght a mercenarie.
He was a shepherd, not a businessman.

And though he holy were and vertuous,   515
And although he was holy and virtuous,

He was to synful men nat despitous,
He was to sinners not merciless,

Ne of his speche daungerous ne digne,
Nor in his speech disdainful or haughty,

But in his techyng discreet and benygne.
But in his teaching quiet and kindly.

To drawen folk to hevene by fairnesse,
To lead people to heaven by uprightness

By good ensample—this was his bisynesse.   520
And good example was his ambition.

But it were any persone obstinat,
But if anyone were obstinate,

What so he were, of heigh or lowe estat,
Whoever he were, of high or low degree,

Hym wolde he snybben sharply for the nonys.
He would reprove him sharply at the time.

A bettre preest I trowe ther nowher noon ys.
A better priest I'm sure does not exist.

He wayted after no pompe and reverence,   525
He expected no pomp or reverence,

Ne maked him a spiced conscience,
Nor considered himself above reproach,

But Cristes loore and his Apostles twelve
But Christ's teaching, and that of his twelve apostles,

He taughte, but first he folwed it hymselve.
He taught, but first he followed it himself.

With hym ther was a Plowman, was his brother,
With him there was a Plowman, his brother,

That hadde ylad of dong ful many a fother;   530
That had carted many a load of dung;

507. This was a not uncommon practice; a priest might engage a substitute in his own parish, and become a chantry priest in London (see 510).

511. To be retained as priest by a guild was also an easy and lucrative position.

Collector of Rents

THE PROLOGUE

[Lines 531-552]

general view of the upper classes toward the peasantry. The Canterbury Tales was begun in 1386 (or '87), and the Peasants' Revolt had taken place in 1381. There was still a good deal of bitterness about the slaughter of these citizens of London whom the rioting peasants regarded as being responsible for their economic plight. As a justice of the peace and a member of parliament, Chaucer might be expected to share the views of the upper class. It is a tribute to his artist's ability to transcend political issues that he gives so admiring an account of a representative of the peasantry. The Plowman's virtues are like his brother: simple and issuing in action. His creed is also simple; in fact, it is the basic obligation of his religion: "God loved he best . . . And thanne his neighebore right as hymselve."

Of the lines devoted to the Miller, notice how many are concerned with physical appearance rather than with more abstract qualities. The opening suggestion of "stout carl" and "Ful big he was of brawn" is carried on in what follows: he is short-armed, broad, a "thikke knarre" with a red spade beard, and even the wart on his nose, with its "tuft of herys/ Rede as the bristles of a sowes erys" is specified. The general effect is of robust physique—compare, for example, the Clerk, who Chaucer says looks hollow.

Millers were most important in the medieval economy and we hear much about them in the stories, poems, and documents of the period. Like Chaucer, many of these sources refer to the millers' dishonesty and sharp practice. The tenants of any manor were obliged to use their lord's mill, and that was operated by the miller, who was thus in an excellent position

A trewe swynkere and a good was he,
A true worker and good was he,

Lyvyng in pees and parfit charitee.
Living in peace and perfect charity.

God loved he best with al his hoole herte
God loved he best with all his whole heart

At alle tymes, thogh him gamed or smerte,
At all times, whether he prospered or suffered,

And thanne his neighebore right as hymselve.   535
And then his neighbor exactly as himself.

He wolde thresshe, and therto dyke and delve,
He would thrash, and also ditch and dig,

For Cristes sake, for every povre wight,
For Christ's sake, for every poor person,

Withouten hire, if it lay in his myght.
Without pay, if it lay in his power.

His tithes payed he ful faire and wel,
His tithes he paid fairly and squarely,

Bothe of his propre swynk and his catel.   540
Both on his own work and his property.

In a tabard he rood upon a mere.
In working clothes he rode upon a mare.

Ther was also a Reve and a Millere,
There was also a Reeve and a Miller,

A Somnour and a Pardoner also,
A Summoner and a Pardoner also,

A Maunciple and myself—ther were namo.
A Manciple and myself—there were no more.

The Millere was a stout carl for the nones;   545
The Miller was a stout fellow (to treat him now);

Ful big he was of brawn and eek of bones.
Large of muscle, and of bones too.

That proved wel, for over al ther he cam,
That had been fully proved, for wherever he went,

At wrastlynge he wolde have alwey the ram.
At wrestling he would always win the prize.

He was short-sholdred, brood, a thikke knarre;
He was short-armed, broad, and thickly built,

Ther was no dore that he nolde heve of harre,   550
There was no door he could not heave off its hinges,

Or breke it at a rennyng with his heed.
Or break it, by running at it with his head.

His berd as any sowe or fox was reed,
His beard was as red as any sow or fox,

The Miller

THE PROLOGUE

to cheat them. This is what Chaucer's Miller does, stealing the flour that should be theirs and getting his fee for milling three times over. It is easy to see how the ironic expression concerning the miller's "thombe of gold" arose, and it probably carries a double significance: that millers were wealthy and that they used a heavy thumb on the scales, to make it seem that they were giving more flour than they were.

Prof. W. C. Curry has examined the way in which the Middle Ages interpreted character according to physiognomy. The fourteenth-century reader would be able to deduce the Miller's character from his physical description. Someone of the Miller's thick-set build was held to be immodest and talkative, as well as violent and easily angered; the flaring nostrils indicate lust; the large mouth ("a greet forneys") means a liar, as well as one much given to profanity. Yet Chaucer is lenient with the Miller, whose sins are venial ones.

While Manciples might be attached to various kinds of institutions, they were most commonly employed by colleges or the Inns of Court, which were very like colleges, since their members were students of the law. This is the point of Chaucer's pretended surprise at 574-75 that such a "lewed" (unlearned) man should be so much more acute than the "heep of lerned men" who were his masters. Chaucer is really contrasting the shrewd practical knowledge of the Manciple with what we can suppose to be the relative naivete of the young legal scholars.

The Manciple was obliged to be shrewd. His duties included accounting for the foodstuffs in the kitchen and buttery, keeping the accounts, and supervising the kitchen and the cook. This last may account for a quarrel that occurs later in the Tales between the Manciple and the Cook. Given their working relationship, there was probably a tradition of dislike between them, which Chaucer dramatized.

And therto brood, as though it were a spade.
And as broad as if it were a spade.

Upon the cop right of his nose he hadde
Right on the tip of his nose he had

A werte, and theron stood a tuft of herys, 555
A wart, and on it was a tuft of hair,

Rede as the bristles of a sowes erys;
Red as the bristles of a sow's ears;

His nosethirles blake were and wyde.
His nostrils were black and large.

A swerd and bokeler bar he by his syde.
A sword and buckler bore he by his side.

His mouth as greet was as a greet forneys.
His mouth was as large as a large furnace.

He was a janglere and a goliardeys, 560
He was a loose talker and a ribald joker,

And that was moost of synne and harlotries.
Mostly concerning sin and indecent stories.

Wel koude he stelen corn and tollen thries;
Well could he steal corn and charge treble;

And yet he hadde a thombe of gold, pardee.
And yet he had a thumb of gold, by heaven.

A whit cote and a blew hood wered he.
A white coat and a blue hood wore he.

A baggepipe wel koude he blowe and sowne, 565
He could play the bagpipe well,

And therwithal he broghte us out of towne.
And with it he accompanied us out of town.

A gentil Maunciple was ther of a temple,
A gentle Manciple was there from an Inn of Court,

Of which achatours myghte take exemple
From whom buyers might take example

For to been wise in byyinge of vitaille;
To learn wisdom in buying provisions;

For wheither that he payde or took by taille, 570
For whether he paid by cash, or by credit,

Algate he wayted so in his achaat,
Always he marketed so carefully,

That he was ay biforn and in good staat.
That he was always ahead and in a good position.

Now is nat that of God a ful fair grace,
Now is not that a fair mercy of God,

That swich a lewed mannes wit shal pace
That such a common man's knowledge shall exceed

The wisdom of an heep of lerned men? 575
The wisdom of a heap of learned men?

The Manciple

560. "goliardeys": the wandering scholars of the twelfth century were known as Goliards, from their leader, Golias. Their poems and songs in Latin were satirical and often indecent.

563. From the proverb "An honest miller has a thumb of gold," meaning that there were no honest millers.

567. "Maunciple": a manciple was a minor employee of an institution, whose principal function was to purchase provisions.
"temple": an Inn of Court. There were four in London—Lincoln's Inn, Gray's Inn, the Inner Temple, and the Middle Temple, the last two taking their names from their buildings, which had belonged to the Knights Templars. They each had about two hundred students who studied common law and liberal arts. Many had no intention of becoming lawyers, but wanted to be able to look after their properties.

THE PROLOGUE

[Lines 576-597]

Chaucer's treatment of the Manciple is relatively flat and colorless, and we neither admire nor disapprove of him. He is a figure reduced to his various functions, not a study in character.

Ring

Of maistres hadde he mo than thries ten,
Of masters had he more than three times ten,

That were of lawe expert and curious,
That were in law expert and skillful,

Of whiche ther were a dozeyne in that hous
Of whom there were a dozen in that house

Worthy to been stywardes of rente and lond
Capable of being stewards of incomes and estates

Of any lord that is in Engelond,   580
Of any lord that is in England,

To make him lyve by his propre good
To enable him to live on his income

In honour dettelees but if he were wood,
Honorably and without debt, unless he were mad,

Or lyve as scarsly as hym list desire,
Or live as frugally as he might want,

And able for to helpen al a shire
And able to help a whole shire

In any caas that myghte falle or happe;   585
In any mischance that might occur;

And yet this Maunciple sette hir aller cappe!
And yet this Manciple could outwit them all!

579. "stywardes": a steward was the chief officer of the manor of a lord, and supervised in his absence.

Although we do not get as extensive a physical description of the Reeve as we did of the Miller, there is enough detail, according to Prof. Curry, to give the contemporary reader some notion of his personality. The Reeve is a "sclendre colerik man," which accords with the belief that those who were thin were also of a choleric humor, easy to anger. But thin people were also held to be sharp-witted, and with excellent memories, and we can see how such qualities would go with the kind of double-dealing the Reeve engages in—no audit could catch him out, and he remembers the mistakes of all his staff. The long legs "Ylik a staf" were evidence of lustfulness, and while this trait does not appear in the Prologue, it does emerge in the tale he tells later in the work.

For us the character of the Reeve is sharp, doubtlessly able to be unpleasant, and endlessly intent on the shrewd and gainful exploitation of his job. It is suggested that he has held this position for a long time (601), and that everything of his lord's is "hoolly in this Reves governyng." He is efficient ("Wel koude he kepe a gerner and a bynne") and it is suggested that he is dishonest in his accounts, yet "Ther was noon auditour koude on him wynne," i.e., no one could

The Reve was a sclendre colerik man.
The Reeve was a slender, choleric man.

His berd was shave as neigh as ever he kan;
His beard was shaven as close as possible;

His heer was by his erys ful round yshorn;
His hair was cut high around his ears;

His top was dokked lyk a preest biforn;   590
He was clipped short in front like a priest;

Ful longe were his legges and ful lene,
His legs were very long and lean,

Ylik a staf, ther was no calf ysene.
Like a stick, no calf was visible.

Wel koude he kepe a gerner and a bynne;
Well could he maintain a granary and bin;

Ther was noon auditour koude on him wynne.
No inspector could get the better of him.

Wel wiste he by the droghte and by the reyn   595
He could predict by the drought and by the rain

The yelding of his seed and of his greyn.
The yield of his seed and grain.

His lordes sheep, his neet, his dayerye,
His lord's sheep, his cattle, his dairy,

587. "Reve": the Reeve was attached to the manor to supervise produce and work, and keep the accounts.

The Reeve

THE PROLOGUE

[Lines 598-620]

catch him out. It is also significant that he knew and remembered all the particular failings of those working beneath him and let them know that he knew. They would never reveal any of his misappropriations and were in fact "adrad of hym as of the deeth." The Reeve is daring in his dishonesties. He has the temerity (or his lord, Chaucer may be implying, has the stupidity) to lend the lord what is really the lord's own property, for which he receives "a thank, and yet a cote and hood."

There is another point of interest about the Reeve, and that is his connection with the Miller. Both are memorably described by Chaucer. One leads the procession of pilgrims, the other stays at the end of it. They are sharply contrasted in appearance, one short and thick, the other long and thin. Later in The Canterbury Tales they have a violent falling-out. The Miller's Tale enrages the Reeve, since it seems to be an attack on him, and he attacks the Miller in his own tale. It also becomes clear that they had known one another before the meeting at the Tabard. This may, of course, be all Chaucer's invention, and it is true that millers and reeves were traditional antagonists, being rivals for power on the estates. Yet Chaucer is so specific about the Miller, and so informative about the Reeve (giving his name, the town he comes from, and even a description of his dwelling), that he may have had two historical characters in mind, and the Miller-Reeve quarrel may have actually occurred, making a topical reference the late fourteenth-century reader would recognize at once.

His swyn, his hors, his stoor, and his pultrye
His swine, his horses, his stock and his poultry

Was hoolly in this Reves governyng,
Were wholly in this Reeve's care,

And by his covenant yaf the rekenyng,　　600
And by agreement he had submitted his accounts,

Syn that his lord was twenty yeer of age.
Ever since his lord was twenty years old.

Ther koude no man brynge hym in arrerage.
No man could find him in arrears.

Ther nas baillif, hierde, nor oother hyne,
There was no supervisor, herdsman or other servant,

That he ne knew his sleighte and his covyne;
Whose cunning and trickery he didn't know;

They were adrad of hym as of the deeth.　　605
They were as frightened of him as of the plague.

His wonyng was ful faire upon an heeth;
His home was in a fair countryside,

With grene trees yshadwed was his place.
With green trees shading the place.

He koude bettre than his lord purchace.
He was a better buyer than his lord.

Ful riche he was astored pryvely.
He had accumulated private wealth.

His lord wel koude he plesen subtilly,　　610
He knew subtle ways of pleasing his lord,

To yeve and lene hym of his owene good,
Giving and loaning him of his own goods,

And have a thank, and yet a cote and hood.
And receiving thanks, and also a coat and hood.

In youthe he hadde lerned a good myster:
In youth he had learned a good trade:

He was a wel good wrighte, a carpenter.
He was a right good worker, a carpenter.

This Reve sat upon a ful good stot,　　615
This Reeve sat upon a very good stallion,

That was a pomely grey and highte Scot.
That was all dappled gray and named Scot.

A long surcote of pers upon he hade,
A long upper-coat of Persian blue he wore,

And by his syde he baar a rusty blade.
And at his side he bore a rusty blade.

Of Northfolk was this Reve of which I telle,
From Norfolk was this Reeve of whom I speak,

Biside a toun men clepen Baldeswelle.　　620
Near a town men call Baldeswell.

14th century costume

611. "his": i.e., the lord's.

43

THE PROLOGUE

[Lines 621-643]

Chaucer has shown us dishonesty in the secular world in the persons of the Miller and the Reeve, but he has not condemned them. He has been harsher on the Friar, who as a religious figure, might have been expected to show more moral rectitude than he does; but the Friar was "A wantowne and a merye," whose humanity is emphasized as well as his immorality. The foibles of the Prioress are also treated with amused indulgence. But for the two clerics who now appear, Chaucer has little sympathy. Both the Summoner and the Pardoner hold offices which lend themselves to abuse, and of this they take full advantage.

The treatment of the Summoner begins with a visual description, but there is more to this than simple visualization. Chaucer presents his physical disorders in a way which suggests inner or spiritual corruption. Chaucer was well versed in medical lore, as we saw in his account of the Doctor, and he chooses the Summoner's ailments with the contemporary medical explanations of them in mind. Prof. Curry cites one authority on the "sawcefleem," the pimpled surface of the face, the Latin term for which is Gutta Rosacea: "Gutta Rosacea be the Latin wordes. In English it is named a sauce fleume face, which is rednes about the nose and the chekes, with small pymples: it is a prevye sign of leprousnes." The medieval diagnosticians were very prone to list all diseases of the skin under leprosy, but the cause of the Summoner's condition is given as drunkenness and excessive eating in youth, the "fleshlye liking" of a diseased woman, and "too hot meates, as long use of strong pepper, or garlike, and of unclean wine . . . ." Chaucer suggests all these gastronomic excesses at 634-35, where he speaks of "garlek, oynons . . . strong wyn reed as blood," and the Summoner's lechery at 652, where the phrase "a fynch . . . koude he pulle"; actually, "to pull a finch," is a fourteenth-century expression meaning to have sexual relations.

Tukked he was as is a frere aboute,
He was girdled up like a friar,

And evere he rood the hyndreste of oure route.
And always he rode last in our group.

A Somnour was ther with us in that place,
There was a Summoner with us in that place,

That hadde a fyr-reed cherubynnes face,
Who had a fire-red cherubim's face,

For sawcefleem he was, with eyen narwe.   625
For pimpled he was, with narrow eyes.

And hoot he was, and lecherous as a sparwe,
And hot he was, and lecherous as a sparrow,

With scaled browes blake and piled berd;
With scabby black brows and scraggly beard;

Of his visage children were aferd.
Of his visage children were afraid.

Ther nas quyksilver, lytarge, ne brymstoon,
There was no quicksilver, lead oxide or brimstone,

Boras, ceruce, ne oille of tartre noon,   630
Borax, white lead, nor cream of tartar,

Ne oinement that wolde clense and byte,
Nor cleansing and caustic ointment,

That hym myghte helpen of his whelkes white,
That could cure him of his white pimples,

Nor of the knobbes sittynge on his chekes.
Nor of the lumps sitting on his cheeks.

Wel loved he garlek, oynons, and eek lekes,
Well loved he garlic, onions, and also leeks,

And for to drynken strong wyn reed as blood.   635
And to drink strong wine, red as blood.

Thanne wolde he speke and crye as he were wood;
Then would he talk and shout as if he were mad;

And whan that he wel dronken hadde the wyn,
And when he had drunk wine heavily,

Thanne wolde he speke no word but Latyn.
Then would he speak no word but Latin.

A fewe termes hadde he, two or thre,
He knew a few terms, two or three,

That he had learned out of som decree—   640
Which he had learned from some decree—

No wonder is, he herde it al the day,
No wonder at that, he heard it all day long,

And eek ye knowen wel how that a jay
And you yourself know how a jay

Kan clepen "Watte" as wel as kan the Pope—
Can say "Wat" as well as the pope can—

623. "Somnour": a summoner was an officer who cited persons to appear in court. In the fourteenth century he was also an officer of the archdeacon, and presided over the archdeacon's court, which had jurisdiction in matrimonial cases and in moral offenses such as adultery and fornication. Bribery was not unknown and other sources beside Chaucer attribute corruption to the summoner.

624. "fyr-reed": cherubs were traditionally painted with red faces in the Middle Ages.

626. Sparrows were proverbially lecherous; the bird was often associated with Venus.

The Summoner

643. "Watte": jays were taught to say "Wat," a diminutive of Walter.

THE PROLOGUE

[Lines 644-666]

Having indicated in this visual way the diseased nature of the Summoner, Chaucer passes on to his behavior. When he is drunk he speaks nothing but Latin, but we find that in contrast to the learning of the Clerk and the Parson he knows only "two or thre" terms and those are learned as a bird might learn, by rote. The familiar Latin tag meaning "What law applies?" was "al his philosophie." The lines that follow at 647-48 are richly sarcastic. Then follows the Summoner's abuse of his ecclesiastical office. He permits licentious behavior (for a price) and indulges in it himself. Although summoners had originally only brought the charge to accused individuals, during the fourteenth century they began to take on some of the function of investigators, or spies, serving the bishop and archdeacon. It is this aspect of their position that leads to the extortionary practices which are denounced by many of the contemporary writers. Excommunication ("Ercedekenes curs") might be performed for a wide variety of sins, such as nonpayment of tithes, sacrilege, desecration, slander, fraud, witchcraft, and so on. It was comparatively easy to indict someone with as inclusive a list as this, which conferred considerable power on the summoner. How Chaucer's Summoner used his power is suggested at 655-60, where the archdeacon's "curs" is either lifted, or never pronounced, because of a payment of money.

As a final touch the Summoner's headgear is as large as an alehouse sign, and his "bokeler" is a huge loaf of bread. These symbols of physical appetite do not suggest robust health (as with the Franklin) but appetite which runs to gluttony.

But whoso koude in oother thyng hym grope,
But if anyone questioned him on anything else,

Thanne hadde he spent al his philosophie; 645
Then he had exhausted all his learning;

Ay *"Questio quid juris"* wolde he crie.
Constantly "Questio quid juris" would he cry.

He was a gentil harlot and a kynde;
He was a gentle rascal and a kind one;

A bettre felawe sholde men noght fynde;
A better companion could not be found;

He wolde suffre, for a quart of wyn,
He would allow, for a quart of wine,

A good felawe to have his concubyn 650
A good fellow to have his mistress

A twelf monthe, and excuse hym atte fulle.
For twelve months, and excuse him fully.

Ful prively a fynch eek koude he pulle.
But he could also take advantage of a girl.

And if he foond owher a good felawe,
And if he found anywhere a good fellow,

He wolde techen him to have noon awe
He would teach him to have no fear

In swich caas of the Ercedekenes curs, 655
In an affair of excommunication,

But if a mannes soule were in his purs,
Unless a man's soul were in his purse,

For in his purs he sholde ypunysshed be.
In that case his purse should be punished.

"Purs is the Ercedekenes helle," saide he.
"The purse is the archdeacon's hell," said he.

But wel I woot he lyed right in dede;
But well I know he most certainly lied;

Of cursyng oghte ech gilty man him drede, 660
Excommunication should be the dread of guilty men,

For curs wol slee right as assoillyng savith,
For excommunication will kill as absolution saves,

And also war him of a *Significavit.*
And also let him beware of a Significavit.

In daunger hadde he at his owene gise
In his own way he had control

The yonge girles of the diocise,
Over the young people of the diocese,

And knew hir conseil, and was al hir reed. 665
And knew their secrets, and was their adviser.

A gerland hadde he set upon his heed
A garland he wore on his head

646. "Questio . . .": "the question is, what law applies"? a common legal expression.

655. "Ercedekenes curs": archdeacon's curse, i.e., excommunication.

Girdle and almoner (purse)

662. "Significavit": the opening word in the writ issued by the authorities to seize a convicted party.

664. "girles": the word may mean young people of either sex.

THE PROLOGUE

[Lines 667-689]

The Pardoner turns out to be a fitting companion for the Summoner and so they join in song. The song the Pardoner sings is a popular love-ditty, but it has been suggested by some scholars that Chaucer gives it to him because of his effeminate nature and that he sings it to the Summoner. This view is to some degree supported by Prof. Curry's findings concerning the medieval view of physiognomy and character. The Pardoner's hair, "yellow as wex" and "smothe" indicates lack of virility, effeminacy of mind, and also deception. However, the effeminacy here may simply be the Pardoner's concern for his clothes and his wish to be in the new mode of fashion. The bright eyes of 684 were supposed to be a sign of folly and immodesty.

The medieval pardoner has as his main occupation the selling of indulgences (the remission of punishment to a repentant sinner), but he might also sell religious relics and preach. The sale of indulgences was an abused practice and finally came to have little to do with the contrition of the sinners. Indulgences were of varying degrees and sold for various prices. Although the money gained through them was meant to be returned to the church, it was obviously easy to adjust the indulgence prices so that not all the money received need be turned in. In addition to this, the people, and especially the simple people, saw the indulgences as a new and easy method of obtaining the remission of sins, and their increased demand increased the pardoner's price. The Pardoner here, with his wallet "Bretful of pardon, comen from Rome al hoot," could expect to do an impressive amount of business in the small English parishes.

As greet as it were for an ale-stake;
As large as an alehouse sign;

A bokeler hadde he maad him of a cake.
A round loaf of bread was his buckler.

With hym ther rood a gentil Pardoner
With him there rode a gentle Pardoner

Of Rouncival, his freend and his compeer, 670
Of Rouncival, his friend and comrade,

That streight was comen fro the court of Rome.
Who had come straight from the court of Rome.

Ful loude he soong, "Com hider, love, to me!"
Full loudly he sang "Come hither, love, to me!"

This Somnour bar to hym a stif burdoun;
The Summoner joined him with a strong bass;

Was nevere trompe of half so greet a soun.
Never was there trumpet half so loud.

This Pardoner hadde heer as yelow as wex, 675
This Pardoner had hair as yellow as wax,

But smothe it heeng as dooth a strike of flex;
But it hung smooth as does a hank of flax;

By ounces henge his lokkes that he hadde,
Such locks as he had hung down thinly,

And therwith he his shuldres overspradde;
And with them he covered his shoulders;

But thynne it lay, by colpons, oon and oon.
But sparsely it lay, by shreds here and there.

But hood for jolitee wered he noon, 680
But, for amusement, he wore no hood,

For it was trussed up in his walet;
For it was packed in his bag;

Hym thoughte he rood al of the newe jet;
He thought he rode in the latest style;

Dischevelee save his cappe he rood al bare.
With hair loose and bareheaded except for his cap.

Swiche glarynge eyen hadde he as an hare.
He had shining eyes like a hare's.

A vernycle hadde he sowed upon his cappe. 685
He had a veronica sewed upon his cap.

His walet lay biforn hym in his lappe,
His bag lay before him on his lap,

Bretful of pardon, comen from Rome al hoot.
Brimful of pardons, come from Rome all hot.

A voys he hadde as smal as hath a goot;
A voice he had as tiny as a goat's;

No berd hadde he, ne nevere sholde have;
No beard had he, nor ever would have;

667. "ale-stake": a horizontal pole extending out from an alehouse, with a garland on the end.

669. "Pardoner": a man authorized to sell papal indulgences, in lieu of other forms of penance. Pardoners were often satirized and criticized for dishonesty.

670. "Rouncival": a convent near Charing Cross, then on the edge of London.

672. Probably a line in a popular song.

The Pardoner

685. "vernycle": a veronica was a copy of St. Veronica's handkerchief, given by her to Christ carrying the cross. It was said to have received the imprint of his face.

THE PROLOGUE

[Lines 690-712]

The practice of selling religious relics was another notorious abuse. Those pardoners who sold false religious objects, vowing that they were real, and kept the money were denounced in a papal edict in 1390. Chaucer makes his Pardoner's wares seem particularly exaggerated. A pillowcase becomes "Oure Lady veyl," while a piece of canvas is St. Peter's sail "whan that he wente/ Upon the see." The "pigges bones" would presumably be peddled as the remains of a saint. Chaucer recounts this with the simple wonder he sometimes affects—"Ne was ther swich another pardoner"—but his meaning is clear, and when we get to the phrase "a noble ecclesiaste" the harsh irony is apparent. Finally there is the Pardoner's facility in song and preaching, which, as a thorough-going confidence man, we might have expected him to have. Here again we note the perversion of the rites of the church, the "lesson" and the "offertorie" used in order "To wynne silver, as he ful wel koude." A contemporary statement (1414) will serve to show the attitude of the reformers within the church to the practices of the pardoners: "Whereas the shameless pardoners sell Indulgences and squander their gains in disgraceful fashion with the prodigal son: but what is more detestable they preach publicly, and pretend falsely that they have full powers of absolving both living and dead alike from punishment and guilt, along with other blasphemies, by means of which they plunder and seduce the people, and drag them down with their own person to the infernal regions of affording them frivolous hope and an audacity to commit sin: therefore let the abuses of this pestilential sect be blotted out from the threshold of the Church."

As smothe it was as it were late yshave;   690
As smooth he was as if he had been shaved;

I trowe he were a geldyng or a mare.
I believe he was a gelding or a mare.

But of his craft, fro Berwyk into Ware,
But in his occupation, from Berwick to Ware,

Ne was ther swich another pardoner.
There was not another such pardoner.

For in his male he hadde a pilwe-beer,
For in his bag he had a pillowcase,

Which that he seyde was Oure Lady veyl;   695
Which he said was Our Lady's veil;

He seyde he hadde a gobet of the seyl
He said he had a small piece of the sail

That Seint Peter hadde whan that he wente
That Saint Peter had when he walked

Upon the see, til Jhesu Crist hym hente.
Upon the sea, until Jesus Christ rescued him.

He hadde a croys of laton, ful of stones,
He had a cross of brass, full of gems,

And in a glas he hadde pigges bones.   700
And in a glass he had pig's bones.

But with thise relikes whan that he fond
But with these relics, whenever he found

A povre person dwellynge upon lond,
A poor parson living in the country,

Upon a day he gat hym moore moneye
Within a day he took in more money

Than that the person gat in monthes tweye;
Than the parson got in two months;

And thus with feyned flaterye and japes,   705
And thus with feigned sincerity and tricks,

He made the person and the peple his apes.
He made monkeys out of the parson and his people.

But trewely to tellen atte laste,
But to tell the truth, all in all,

He was in chirche a noble ecclesiaste;
He was in church a noble ecclesiastic;

Wel koude he rede a lesson or a storie,
He knew how to read a lesson or a story,

But alderbest he song an offertorie;   710
But best of all he sang an offertory;

For wel he wiste whan that song was songe,
For well he knew when that song was sung,

He moste preche and wel affile his tonge
He must preach and sharpen his tongue

692. The phrase means from one end of England to the other.

698. "hym hente": the reference is either to Christ's extending a helping hand to Peter when the latter walked on the water and became afraid or to the fact that Peter was a fisherman before joining Christ.

Game of skill

709. "lesson": passage from the Bible or the Fathers read in the service; a "storie" is several such connected lessons.

710. "offertorie": a chant preparatory to the ceremonial offering of the Bread and Wine, at which time the people made their offerings.

THE PROLOGUE

[Lines 713-735]

The introduction and description of the pilgrims, with the exception of the "Host" of the inn, is at an end. In order to recall his readers to the dramatic setting of the Tales Chaucer returns to the point at which the Prologue began, "In Southwerk at this gentil hostelrye/ That highte the Tabard, faste by the Belle." He then explains his method of narration. Here again Chaucer assumes his pose of the simple man, devoid of literary pretensions, who will simply entertain his reader. The reader's "curteisye" will, Chaucer hopes, keep him from disapproving too much of the "vileynye" of some of the stories that are to come. He will "pleynly speke in this matere" and attempt to recapture the tale as he heard it, no matter how "rudeliche" the language may be. The language and situations in some of the tales to come are "rudeliche," and Chaucer here provides a graceful warning to that effect, but he is able to summon both Christ and Plato in his support, thus subtly suggesting that he does, after all, know what he is doing. This tone of mock-modesty continues through the passage and its humor comes, perhaps, from the spectacle of a great technician apologizing for his lack of technique and a brilliant artist telling us not to mind his mistakes: "My wit is short, ye may wel understonde."

To wynne silver, as he ful wel koude;
To win silver, as he well knew how;

Therefore he song the murierly and loude.
Therefore he sung so merrily and loud.

Now have I told you soothly, in a clause,   715
Now I have told you truly, in brief,

Th'estaat, th'array, the nombre, and eek the cause
The status, the dress, the number, and also the cause

Why that assembled was this compaignye
Of the gathering of this company

In Southwerk at this gentil hostelrye
In Southwark at this fine inn

That highte the Tabard, faste by the Belle.
Called the Tabard, close to the Bell.

But now is tyme to yow for to telle   720
But now it is time to tell you

How that we baren us that ilke nyght,
What we did that same night,

Whan we were in that hostelrie alyght;
On which we came to that inn;

And after wol I telle of our viage
And afterward I will tell you of our journey,

And al the remenaunt of oure pilgrimage.
And the remainder of our pilgrimage.

But first I pray yow of youre curteisye,   725
But first I beg you out of your courtesy,

That ye n'arette it nat my vileynye,
That you do not ascribe it to my ill breeding,

Thogh that I pleynly speke in this matere,
Even though I speak plainly in this narration,

To telle yow hir wordes and hir cheere,
To tell you their words and their behavior,

Ne thogh I speke hir wordes proprely.
Even though I repeat their exact words.

For this ye knowen al so wel as I: 730
For this you know as well as I:

Who so shal telle a tale after a man,
Whoever tells another man's story,

He moot reherce, as neigh as evere he kan,
Must reproduce, as exactly as he can,

Everich a word, if it be in his charge,
Every word, if his memory serves,

Al speke he never so rudeliche and large,
However crude and free his language,

Or ellis he moot telle his tale untrewe,   735
Or else he tells his tale untruly,

719. "the Belle": another tavern.

Pendant

THE PROLOGUE

[Lines 736-758]

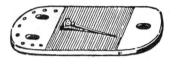

Writing tablet

The Host (whose name, we discover later, is Harry Bailly) does not really come into his own until the telling of tales begins, but his character is suggested here. He is a large, commanding, genial man. His manner is direct and sensible, he is efficient, and, Chaucer says, he is fit "For to been a marchal in an halle." This is high praise, since "an halle" is a lord's manor, where the marshal served as the household's chief organizer for the guests and their food and drink. There is evidence to suggest that Chaucer is praising a real innkeeper here, since a Harry Bailly did keep an inn in Southwark in Chaucer's time. The Subsidy Roll of Southwark for 1380-81 records one "Henricus Bailiff, Ostyler," and there are several other references to him in various other connections.

The Host's importance in the Prologue lies in his proposal to the pilgrims that they entertain themselves on the journey to Canterbury and back by telling tales. After seeing to his guests "vitaille" and "wyn" (and also attending to the "reckenynges," for he is always a practical man) he explains the terms of his proposal. It calls for a hundred and twenty tales, since each pilgrim is to tell two stories on the journey to Canterbury and two more on the way back to Southwark, where the teller of the best tale is to be given dinner at the cost of all ("Here in this place" he adds, still practical).

Or feyne thyng, or fynde wordes newe.
Or invent things, or find new words.

He may nat spare althogh he were his brother;
He may spare no one, not even his brother;

He moot as wel seye o word as another.
He is as bound to say one word as another.

Crist spak hymself ful brode in holy writ,
Christ Himself spoke broadly enough in holy writ,

And wel ye woot no vileynye is it.   740
And you know well that it is not immoral.

Eek Plato seith, whoso kan him rede,
Plato also says, for those who can read him,

The wordes mote be cosyn to the dede.
That words should be cousin to the deed.

Also I pray yow to foryeve it me,
Also I beg you to forgive me,

Al have I nat set folk in hir degree
If I have not placed people in their rank,

Here in this tale as that they sholde stonde.   745
Here in this tale in the order that they should be.

My wit is short, ye may wel understonde.
My brains are weak, you can well understand.

Greet cheere made oure Hoost us everichon,
Our Host gave each of us a great welcome,

And to the soper sette he us anon.
And set us down to supper forthwith.

He served us with vitaille at the beste;
He served us with the best of food;

Strong was the wyn, and wel to drynke us leste.   750
Strong was the wine, and we were in a mood to drink.

A semely man oure Hooste was withalle
Our Host was a man altogether fit

For to been a marchal in an halle.
To have been a marshall in a dining hall.

A large man he was, with eyen stepe;
A large man he was, with bright eyes;

A fairer burgeys was ther noon in Chepe,
There was no finer citizen in Cheapside,

Boold of his speche, and wys, and wel ytaught,   755
Bold of speech, and sensible, and well educated,

And of manhood hym lakkede right naught.
And he lacked nothing of real manhood.

Eek therto he was right a murye man,
As well as this he was a merry man,

And after soper pleyen he bigan,
And after supper he began to jest,

14th century costume

752. "marchal": the marshall was the person of authority in serving meals. He directed the servants and quelled disturbances if necessary.

754. "Chepe": Cheapside, a main thoroughfare in Chaucer's London, and a center of commerce.

THE PROLOGUE

[Lines 759-781]

Through the host, Chaucer has proposed an immense narrative task for himself that was never finished. Of the one hundred and twenty tales only twenty were completed, seven of the thirty pilgrims tell no tales at all, and we part with the pilgrimage before it reaches Canterbury. This simply means that the Prologue (as we might expect) was written before any, or very many, of the tales were completed.

We notice how pleasantly, yet at the same time how deftly and with what command, the Host takes over the direction of the pilgrims. There is no debate about his plan. Those who want to "stonden at my juggement," he says, "Hoolde up youre hondes withouten moore speche"—and they do. From this point on in The Canterbury Tales the host will be chairman, stage manager, judge, and choric commentator for the group's succession of fictional recitals. Now he arranges the drawing of lots to decide who will tell the first story. Does he 'arrange' the choice of the Knight? Certainly he is capable of it, and Chaucer leaves the matter in doubt (843-44). In any case the Knight steps forward to begin his tale, and the greatest narrative performance in English literature is underway.

And spak of myrthe amonges othere thynges,
And spoke of pleasure among other things,

Whan that we hadde maad oure rekenynges, 760
After we had settled our bills,

And seyde thus, "Now, lordynges, trewely,
And spoke thus, "Now, gentlemen, truly,

Ye been to me right welcome, hertely;
You are heartily welcome here;

For by my trouthe, if that I shal nat lye,
For by my troth, if I don't tell a lie,

I saugh nat this yeer so murye a compaignye
I have not seen this year so merry a company

At ones in this herberwe as is now. 765
At once in this inn as at present.

Fayn wolde I doon yow myrthe, wiste I how.
I should like to provide pleasure for you, if I knew how.

And of a myrthe I am right now bythoght
And a pastime has just occurred to me

To doon yow ese, and it shal coste noght.
To give you pleasure, and it will cost nothing.

Ye goon to Caunterbury—God yow speede;
You go to Canterbury—God speed you;

The blisful martir quite yow youre meede. 770
May the blessed martyr reward you.

And wel I woot as ye goon by the weye,
And well I know as you go along,

Ye shapen yow to talen and to pleye,
You plan to tell tales and amuse yourselves,

For trewely, confort ne myrthe is noon
For truly, there is no comfort nor mirth

To ride by the weye domb as a stoon;
In riding along silent as a stone;

And therfore wol I maken yow disport, 775
And therefore I shall create a diversion,

As I seyde erst, and doon yow som confort.
As I said before, and give you some comfort.

And if yow liketh alle, by oon assent,
And if you all agree, by common consent,

For to stonden at my juggement,
To be ruled by my judgment,

And for to werken as I shal yow seye,
And to proceed as I shall explain,

Tomorwe whan ye riden by the weye, 780
Tomorrow when you go on your way,

Now by my fader soule that is deed,
Now by my father's soul who is dead,

French shoe

THE PROLOGUE

[Lines 782-804]

14th century costume

But ye be murye I wol yeve yow myn heed!
If you are not merry I will give you my head!

Hoolde up youre hondes withouten moore speche."
Hold up your hands without more talk."

   Oure conseil was nat longe for to seche;
   Our decision was not hard to find;

Us thoughte it was nat worth to make it wys,   785
We did not think it worth deliberating over,

And graunted hym withouten moore avys,
And agreed with him without further consideration,

And bad him seye his voirdit as hym leste.
And asked him to give his verdict as it pleased him.

   "Lordynges," quod he, "now herkneth for the
      beste;
   "Gentlemen," he said, "now listen with good will;

But taak it nought, I prey yow, in desdeyn.
And take it not, I beg you, disdainfully.

This is the poynt, to speken short and pleyn,   790
This is the point, to speak briefly and plainly,

That ech of yow, to shorte with oure weye
That each of you, to shorten our way

In this viage, shal telle tales tweye—
On this journey, shall tell two tales—

To Caunterbury-ward, I mene it so—
En route to Canterbury, I mean to say—

And homward he shal tellen othere two,
And two more on the way homeward,

Of aventures that whilom have bifalle;   795
Of adventures that have once happened;

And which of yow that bereth hym best of alle—
And whichever of you does the best of all—

That is to seyn, that telleth in this caas
That is to say, that tells in this contest

Tales of best sentence and moost solaas—
The most significant and amusing tales—

Shal have a soper at oure aller cost,
Shall be given dinner at the expense of all,

Here in this place, sittynge by this post,   800
Here in this place, sitting by this post,

Whan that we come agayn fro Caunterbury.
When we return from Canterbury.

And for to make yow the moore mury,
And to make you more merry,

I wol myselven goodly with yow ryde,
I will myself gladly ride with you,

Right at myn owene cost, and be youre gyde;
Even at my own expense, and be your guide;

Anelace (purse)

794. The plan which calls for four tales from each pilgrim was never completed.

51

THE PROLOGUE

[Lines 805-827]

Altar cross

And who so wole my juggement withseye   805
And whoever opposes my judgment

Shal paye al that we spenden by the weye.
Shall pay all that we spend along the way.

And if ye vouche sauf that it be so,
And if you promise that it will be so,

Tel me anon, withouten wordes mo,
Tell me at once, without more words,

And I wol erly shape me therefore."
And I will prepare myself accordingly."

This thyng was graunted and oure othes swore   810
This thing was granted and our oaths sworn

With ful glad herte, and preyden hym also
With entirely glad hearts, and we begged him too

That he wolde vouche sauf for to do so,
That he would agree to do his part,

And that he wolde been oure governour,
And that he would be our director,

And of oure tales juge and reportour,
And remember and judge our tales,

And sette a soper at a certeyn pris,   815
And plan a dinner at a certain price,

And we wol reuled been at his devys
And we would be ruled by his direction

In heigh and lowe; and thus by oon assent
In great and small things; and thus by general consent

We been acorded to his juggement.
We fell in with his plan.

And therupon the wyn was fet anon;
And at that the wine was quickly fetched;

We dronken and to reste wente echon,   820
And we drank and each went to bed,

Withouten any lenger taryynge.
Without any further delay.

Amorwe whan that day bigan to sprynge,
Next morning when day began to break,

Up roos oure Hoost and was oure aller cok,
Up rose our Host and was rooster for us all,

And gadred us togidre in a flok,
And gathered us together in a flock,

And forth we riden, a litel moore than paas,   825
And forth we rode, slightly faster than a walk,

Unto the wateryng of Seint Thomas;
As far as the watering-place of Saint Thomas;

And there oure Hoost bigan his hors areste,
And there our Host slowed down his horse,

Drawing from brass effigy

826. "wateryng": a watering place for horses at the second milestone on the road to Canterbury.

52

THE PROLOGUE

[Lines 828-850]

And seyde, "Lordynges, herkneth if yow leste.
And said, "Gentlemen, listen if you please.

Ye woot youre forward and I it yow recorde;
You know your agreement and I remind you of it;

If even-song and morwe-song accorde, 830
If evening and morning are in agreement,

Lat see now who shal telle the firste tale.
Let us see now who shall tell the first tale.

As evere mote I drynke wyn or ale,
If ever again I drink wine or ale,

Who so be rebel to my juggement
Whoever rebels against my decision

Shal paye for al that by the wey is spent.
Shall pay for all that by the way is spent.

Now draweth cut er that we ferrer twynne; 835
Now draw lots, before we go farther;

He which that hath the shorteste shal bigynne.
Whoever draws the shortest shall begin.

Sire Knyght," quod he, "my mayster and my lord,
Sir Knight," said he, "my master and my lord,

Now draweth cut, for that is myn accord.
Now draw your lot, for that is my ruling.

Cometh neer," quod he, "my lady Prioresse,
Come closer," said he, "my lady Prioress,

And ye, sire Clerk, lat be youre shamefastnesse, 840
And you, sir Clerk, forget your bashfulness,

Ne studieth noght. Ley hond to, every man!"
Do not deliberate. Hands out, every man!"

Anon to drawen every wight bigan,
And so everyone began to draw,

And shortly for to tellen as it was,
And to speak briefly, as it happened,

Were it by aventure or sort or cas,
Whether by adventure or luck or chance,

The sothe is this, the cut fil to the Knyght, 845
The fact is this, the lot fell to the Knight,

Of which ful blithe and glad was every wight,
Which was pleasing to everyone,

And telle he moste his tale, as was resoun,
And tell his tale he must, as was right,

By forward and by composicioun,
By agreement and according to plan,

As ye han herd. What nedeth wordes mo?
As you have heard. Why use more words?

And whan this goode man saugh that it was so, 850
And when this good man saw that it was so,

14th century costume

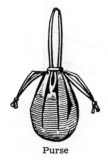

Purse

53

THE PROLOGUE

[Lines 851-858]

As he that wys was and obedient
Since he was wise and willing

To kepe his forward by his free assent,
To keep his agreement by free consent,

He seyde, "Syn I shal begynne the game,
He said, "Since I am to begin the game,

What, welcome be the cut, a Goddes name!
Why, welcome be the lot, in God's name.

Now lat us ryde, and herkneth what I seye."   855
Now let us ride, and listen to what I say."

And with that word we ryden forth oure weye,
And with that word we rode forth on our way,

And he bigan with right a murye cheere
And he began in great good spirits

His tale anon, and seyde as ye may heere.
His tale at once, and said what you may hear.

Dinner at the Tabard Inn, Southwark

NOTES

NOTES